DEADLY
INNOCENCE?

DEADLY INNOCENCE?

ROBERT PERSKE

Abingdon Press
Nashville

Deadly Innocence?

Copyright © 1995 by Robert Perske and Martha Perske

All rights reserved.

This book is printed on recycled, acid-free paper.

Library of Congress Cataloging-in-Publication Data

Perske, Robert.
    Deadly innocence? / Robert Perske.
       p.   cm.
    Includes bibliographical references and index.
    ISBN 0-687-00615-5 (alk. paper)
    1. Arridy, Joe, 1815–1939.   2. Mentally handicapped offenders—
Colorado—Biography.   3. Murderers—Colorado—Biography.
4. Capital punishment—Colorado.   5. Mentally handicapped and crime—
Colorado.   I. Title.
HV6533.C6P47   1995
364.1'523'0978855—dc20

95-35089

Excerpts from the poem "The Clinic" are used by the permission of its author, Marguerite Young.

95 96 97 98 99 00 01 02 03 04 — 10 9 8 7 6 5 4 3 2 1

MANUFACTURED IN THE UNITED STATES OF AMERICA

For Martha, my pal

ACKNOWLEDGMENTS

I am indebted to a number of people who inspired, aided, and supported this journey:

Friends and Colleagues

Don Connery, Richard Dieter, Leigh Dingerson, Rosemary Dybwad, Gunnar Dybwad, James Ellis, John Finn, Stephen Greenspan, Kristine B. Kendrick, Brian Lensink, Ruth Luckasson, Martha Perske, Jean Mercier, Dolores Norley, Lou Shaw, J. David Smith, Diann Rust-Tierney, Richard Voorhees, Miriam Weintraub, Karima Wicks, Robert R. Williams, and Marguerite Young.

Archivist and Historians

Judy Prosser-Armstrong (Regional History Division, Museum of Western Colorado, Grand Junction); Jean Brainerd (Wyoming State Archives, Main Library, Cheyenne); Joanne Dodds (District Archives of the Public Library, Pueblo, Colorado); Watt Espy (Capital Punishment Project, Headland, Alabama); Cara Fisher (Local History Center of the Public Library, Canon City, Colorado); Linda Watson (Colorado State Archives, Denver)

The Darien Library Research and Assistance Desk

Mary Fox, Valerie Fredericks, Sylvia Hill, Blanche Parker, Janie Rhein, and Maura Ritz. Library Pages: Philippe Monin and Sue Skerrett.

CONTENTS

1

THE POEM

As soon as my friend sociologist Richard Voorhees spied the poem, he moved fast. He had discovered the poem in a musty, out-of-print book during a research pursuit in New York City's Greenwich Village. He typed it up, scrawled "I'll bet this grabs you" at the top of the page, and dropped it in the mail (Voorhees, 1992). As soon as I received it, I read the first stanza.

Then I read it again:

> The warden wept before the lethal beans
> Were dropped that night in the airless room,
> Fifty faces peering against glassed screens,
> A clinic crowd outside the tomb.

I read on. In the poem, the warden watches a convict playing joyfully with a toy train. Then, in obvious anguish, he writes "a sorry letter."

"The man you kill tonight," he writes, "is six years old. He has no idea why he dies."

Later, the warden stands in a "stony corridor"; he weeps and wonders who will "shut the final door" on the convict and "who will watch the fume upon his face?"

In the meantime, paying no attention to all the grim ritualistic preparations going on around him, the doomed man goes right on racing his toy train over "its tinny tracks." He plays with that train right up until the warden and other officials come for him, take him to a special chamber, and snuff out his life.

2

THE QUERY

I read the poem again and again. I struggled with its imagery. I wondered whether the story of the saddened warden and the toy-train-loving convict was true. So I tracked down the poet, Marguerite Young, who still lived in Greenwich Village. She said she wrote the poem and published it in 1944, in response to a newspaper article she had read many years ago. She couldn't recall the name of the convict or where the execution had taken place.

I sent the poem to Watt Espy, the director of the Capital Punishment Project in Headland, Alabama. As the keeper of records for almost 19,000 people executed since colonial times in America, he agreed to do a search for me.

A few days later, Espy responded with a packet containing a few old newsclips and detective magazines. From them, I learned that the convict who played with the toy train was small (five-feet-four, 130 pounds), Joe Arridy, 23 years old. He was born in Pueblo, Colorado, in 1915, shortly after his parents had immigrated from Syria. The newsclips said that he was "feebleminded," and at age 10, he had been sent to the Colorado State Home and Training School for Mental Defectives at Grand Junction.

At age 21, Arridy was arrested for vagrancy in the Cheyenne, Wyoming, railroad yards. Interrogated by a sheriff, he confessed to the August 15, 1936, rape and ax murder of 15-year-old Dorothy Drain in Pueblo, Colorado. The sheriff telephoned the Pueblo police and told them he had cracked their case.

The news of Arridy's confession, however, was received by the Pueblo police with surprise because they were hard at work investigating and interrogating 35-year-old Frank Aguilar for the same crime. Furthermore, they had discovered the murder weapon, a hatchet head, hidden in Aguilar's home. Hearing that, the Cheyenne sheriff decided to interrogate Arridy again. This time, Arridy stated that he did not commit the crime alone.

Both Arridy and Aguilar were charged with first-degree murder. Each received separate trials. Neither attended the other's trial as a witness, and both were convicted and sentenced to death.

Justice came quickly for Aguilar. He was sentenced on February 3, 1937, and died in the gas chamber at the Colorado State Penitentiary at Canon City on August 13, 1937—just three days short of a year after the crime.

Arridy's trial was swift, too. He was defended by a court-appointed attorney who conducted no investigation and called three psychiatrists and one medical doctor as expert witnesses. These witnesses, all failing to discuss the man's guilt or innocence, tried to convince the jury that Arridy was insane. Arridy was sentenced on June 25, 1937, and sent to the penitentiary at Canon City to await execution. After the sentence, however, Denver lawyer Gail L. Ireland picked up the case and filed one appeal after another on Arridy's behalf. He obtained nine stays in less than a year and a half.

The warden was Roy Best, who became friends with Arridy. When reporters wanted to know how Arridy was doing in prison, Best usually began by saying, "Joe Arridy is the happiest man who ever lived on death row."

It was Best who supplied toys, picture books, and other items for Arridy to play with in his cell. As he played, his unabashed laughter and shouts of glee could be heard throughout the cell block. Best gave the toy train to Arridy as his last Christmas present.

On January 6, 1939, it was Best who supervised the shutting of the gas-chamber door and gave the signal for the lethal beans to drop.

3

THE CALLING

I was raised in Colorado. Arridy drew me back from the East Coast to familiar territory—Denver, Pueblo, Grand Junction, Colorado Springs, Canon City, and across the border to Cheyenne. He set me to searching through microfilms of *The Denver Post*, the *Rocky Mountain News*, *The Pueblo Chieftain*, the Grand Junction *Daily Sentinel*, *The Canon City Daily Record*, and the *Wyoming State Tribune—Cheyenne State Leader*. Day after day, I watched old newspapers race across the projection screens until double doses of Dramamine were needed to fight the vertigo. I stayed at it until a copy of every news story that could be found was in my possession.

By then, my scanty, self-rehearsed sketch of Arridy's life and death was enough to win the assistance of good archivists and volunteer helpers in each of the major cities. We knew that after all these years, there would be gaps in the story. And yet, these thoughtful helpers discovered items I never could have found—court records, school records, death notices, institutional records.

I tried to obtain trial transcripts from the Pueblo County Court where Arridy's trial was held. But the clerks were convinced that the records surely had been destroyed by now. Then Linda Watson, an archivist in Denver, tracked down *Colorado v Arridy* (1937), as well as the briefs and transcripts of *Arridy v Colorado* (1938)—every page!

I knew about Warden Roy Best. I had met that colorful rancher and rodeo-cowboy turned penal-expert in 1946. The meeting amounted to a brief delivery of equipment and a quick handshake while I was working for the communications division of the Colorado State Patrol. After that, my ears were perked for stories about this unique and unrepeatable warden. Later, it was Best's care and common sense that made Joe Arridy really come alive to me—so much so that I began dreaming about the little guy.

I have spent more than thirty-five years working for and supporting people like Joe Arridy—first as an institutional worker, later in community services, and more recently as a writer and supporter in their own neighborhoods. Some of my most loyal and enjoyable friends cannot read or write or speak plainly. Some may never walk. I have watched as our nation's standards of decency have evolved until many we once rejected have now become valued members of their own neighborhoods.

As for executions, I've been around a few. For the past six years, I have followed and written about vulnerable people on death rows—many with mental retardation, mental illness, and brain damage. Quite often, they confessed too easily to heinous crimes with little physical evidence to back up their admissions. Some, of course, were guilty of the crimes. Others were not. I watched some of them walk out of prison. I watched others walk to their death.

So when I read the poem and the early reports about Joe Arridy, I felt my adrenalin surge.

4

BESSEMER

It was 1909, and the word was out in tiny Berosha on the slopes of Mount Lebanon: "Life is better in America." That word couldn't have come at a better time for this gritty little community of Maronite Christians. For though they lived high up, life for them had touched bottom.

Berosha, on Mount Lebanon, was part of a much larger Syria that had touched the eastern end of the Mediterranean Sea. The land formed a bridge between three continents—Africa, Asia, and Europe—and for thousands of years had served as a marching ground for conquerors and religious crusaders. When one considers the marauding rulers and propagators of faith and frenzy, all impinging their wills on the Syrians, one suddenly becomes aware of a heritage that could give a historian a headache.

Earlier, the Maronite community had lived a good life in the lowlands on better soil. But the conquering forces kept them on the move until they ended up on the side of Mount Lebanon. There crops could be planted only in the less fertile soil found between porous, water-absorbing limestone rocks. The controllers were the Ottoman Turks, under the worst leader of all time, Sultan Abdul Hamid II. To the Maronites, he was known as Abdul Hamid the Damned, and his local lieutenant was called The Butcher, indicating what happened when anyone failed to come up with the tax money for the sultan.

Then a small number of Berosha's citizens broke away and headed for the New World. Some settled in Pueblo, Colorado, where they found work in the town's principal industry, the Colorado Fuel and Iron Works. These intrepid pioneers did indeed see that life was better in America, and they invited their friends and relatives in the old country to come and see for themselves.

At the time, CF&I was burgeoning, like hundreds of other factories then being energized by the great Industrial Revolution. They needed unskilled workers badly. The Contract Labor Law passed by Congress in 1885, however, prohibited the companies from going to foreign lands and signing up workers. So CF&I did everything it could to advise and support the ethnic inviters.

Henry Arridy heard the word in Berosha and decided to make the trip. Being a short, sinewy, nervous person of approximately 23 years (he never seemed able to decide on his real age) always dependent upon authority figures around him for advice, he was guided by his elders to Patmos, Greece, where he boarded the S.S. *Martha Washington*. The

Washington was chosen because it was bound for Philadelphia—not New York and Ellis Island.

Corporate managers did everything they could to help Pueblo's ethnic communities to steer their loved ones around Ellis Island. They had learned the hard way that immigration officials there had become "too quick with the chalk." As many as 15,000 immigrants, most with no jobs or specific destinations, moved daily through that "Isle of Tears," where two out of every ten were rejected:

> [The immigrants] moved in a single file through a stockyard maze of passageways and under the eye of a doctor in a blue uniform who had in his hand a piece of chalk. He was a tough instant diagnostician. He would look at the hands, the hair, the faces and rap out a few questions. He might spot a panting old man with purple lips, and he would chalk on his back a capital "H" for suspected heart disease. Any facial blotches, a hint of gross eczema brought forth a chalked "F" for facial rash. Children in arms were made to stand down to see if they rated an "L" for the limp of rickets or some other deficiency disease. There was one chalk mark that every family dreaded, for it guaranteed certain deportation. It was a circle with a cross in the middle, and it indicated "feeble-minded" (Cooke, 1975, pp. 282-83).

Henry Arridy's landing in Philadelphia on July 5, 1909, was nothing like one on Ellis Island. Since he couldn't read or write, he was helped with his immigration papers. He was also helped to file his first set of U.S. citizenship papers—even though he later failed to file the rest of the required papers. Then he was on his way to Pueblo, where a relative helped him find a job in one of CF&I's foundries. His job was shoveling the packing sand into foundry molds, in preparation for the pouring of molten metals.

The 1920 census shows that Mary Arridy, approximately 22, joined her husband three years later, after debarking in Philadelphia and undergoing the same process. It is not known where the couple lived, but she became pregnant immediately. A death record shows that their firstborn son, also named Joe, died on July 30, 1913, after only two months.

The second Joe Arridy was born in Pueblo on April 29, 1915. His earthly journey toward execution began in a small rented bungalow at 1042 Elm Street, within a section known as Bessemer.

Joe was a healthy, well-formed baby. Later photographs (except for the police mugshots taken at the time of the crime) show him to be winsome and attractive. Somehow, his pleasant, trusting face, his lean, short frame, his dark eyes and shiny black hair, and his relaxed, hands-in-pockets posture always reminded me of Dustin Hoffman, the actor. In no case did his photos show any signs of developmental disability.

The infant Joe lived on a block where at every daybreak, except holidays and Sundays, most of the men left their homes wearing bib overalls and carrying lunch pails. They paraded two blocks south on Elm Street to Northern Boulevard and walked east, marching with hundreds of others over the railroad tracks to the Colorado Fuel and Iron Works grounds, with its massive buildings and towering smokestacks. Those stacks—never ceasing to fill the sky with black smoke—made it easy for anyone scanning the eastern Colorado plains from the Rocky Mountains to pinpoint Pueblo, especially the Bessemer District.

But Bessemer was no spacious suburb. According to Pueblo historian Joanne Dodds:

The same men who owned the steel works had also owned the real estate company that laid out Bessemer. The small lots and closely packed houses were for industrial workers who after 12-hour days in the mill had no strength left to water and mow lawns. A beer at the neighborhood bar to ease their tired muscles was more appealing (Dodds, 1995).

As children were born in the small houses, their presence changed the character of the crowded, closeknit neighborhood. After supper on warm evenings, spring-tethered screendoors squeaked open and slammed loudly up and down the street. Children poured out of bungalows and ran full-speed to their favorite meeting spot in the middle of the street. They chose up sides and played street games. Later, after the supper dishes had been washed, parents appeared on their front porches and shouted greetings across the street and on both sides. After dark, the kids engaged in the best game of all—hide and seek. The loud counting, the seeking, the wild dashes to home base, and the arguments over who touched base first continued until parents called their sons and daughters home to bed. Nobody locked their doors.

Life was better in Bessemer for most people. But I soon learned that it wasn't that way for the Arridys.

5

INCREDIBLE DIVERSITY

Picture a dry, almost desert-like plain on the eastern slope of the Rocky Mountains. At this spot, the Arkansas river flows out of the mountains from the west and meets Fountain Creek as it meanders along the foothills from the north. For years, the Utes lived a free-spirited life, camping, hunting, and fishing in the area. Spanish explorers stopped for a while at this river junction in the 18th century. Colonel Zebulon Pike spent time there in 1806, after getting a close look at one of the most magnificent mountains he had ever seen—a peak destined to become his namesake. After that, incredibly diverse groups of people came together on this spot during the next hundred years. At first, some groups responded to other groups as oil does to water.

In 1842, Fort Pueblo was established on this spot as a meeting place for traders and members of the Ute nation—only to be wiped out on Christmas Day, 1854. According to the April 30, 1915, edition of *The Pueblo Chieftain,* the Utes came to Christmas festivities at the fort, and became so intoxicated that they massacred all the whites, except for two young lads who escaped.

By 1858, prospectors—most of them with English, Irish, German, and Scandinavian backgrounds—stopped at local stores on the river junction to purchase panning supplies before rushing into the Rocky Mountains in search of gold. More people from diverse backgrounds settled in Pueblo when the railroad was established fourteen years later.

As soon as the Colorado Fuel & Iron Works was founded in 1881, the great need for unskilled laborers set off a massive influx of immigrants, many from countries east and south of Germany.

By the time Joe Arridy was born, on April 29, 1915, Pueblo had a population of 58,464. It was a salad bowl of ethnic communities—each clinging tightly to its own cultural values:

Isolated by choice and by cultures, immigrants lived in secure neighborhoods. Groceries were purchased from the store a few doors away. The owner was your nationality and was always willing to extend credit until pay day. For entertainment there were the lodges and fraternal organizations of your own culture. And you were careful not to fall behind in paying the ten-cent burial insurance fee each week that would provide you with a decent funeral in a land of strangers. On Sunday, the family went to one of the national churches where the priest spoke your language and helped the children remember your customs.

In this New World you had to be tough. Immigrants stayed within their neighborhoods. If a stranger asked you a question in English, you acted as if you didn't understand even if you did. And if your neighbor had a problem with "an American," you minded your own business (Dodds, 1995).

Then, slowly but surely, some people from different cultures dared to deal with, be friendly with, and curious about one another. With time and respect, and some anguish, they adjusted to the differences—and were better off for doing so. Pueblo was better off, too. There were those, however, who simply could not make such shifts, but many of their children did.

The ideal was epitomized in some of the literature and plays of the day. For example, the play "Abie's Irish Rose," the story of a Jewish husband and an Irish wife, received rave reviews in the May 24, 1922, *New York Times*. Later, it was expanded into a weekly radio serial drama that drew the whole family around a gothic Philco or a crystal set, with its talking headset placed just right in a metal mixing bowl on the kitchen table.

The city's leaders recognized the need to take the very best from all these diverse Old World cultures and somehow meld them all into one glorious New World citizenry. On the day Joe Arridy was born, *The Pueblo Chieftain* used every wooing note in its editorial toolbox to get *all* Pueblans together for the next Saturday's May Day celebration in the city park:

> The best spring festival ever held in Pueblo will be celebrated at City park on Saturday next. There will be four main features of the festival: first, a series of competitions in athletics, music and declamation among the school children of the city, with simple and inexpensive municipal prizes to those excelling in these contests; second, a popular outdoor picnic luncheon, in which every family in the city is invited to participate; third, a pageant illustrative of the history of Pueblo from the earliest pioneer to the present, shown in a series of nine tableaux; fourth, an open air folk-dance and play festival....
>
> There is in this idea and in the earnest work of those who have labored for its success the material for a regular Pueblo annual festival, unique in character, attractive in feature, and of a nature to arouse a very wide public interest in it.
>
> We hope that every family in Pueblo who have children in any of the schools of the city will make it a point to take their picnic luncheons to City park next Saturday and that all others who can will join the crowd at Pueblo's biggest and best Spring Festival.

The climactic epochs in the pageant dealt with the completion of the Denver & Rio Grande railroad (1872), the establishment of the Colorado Fuel and Iron Works (1881), and the present nature of togetherness in Pueblo. "Pueblo today," *The Chieftain* said, "is a cosmopolitan city, including among its inhabitants many nationalities and peoples whom it is uniting under one flag and for the service of Great America."

But the Arridy family may have been a little too different. Somehow, its members didn't seem to put down roots in their own culture. And the larger city interests only bewildered them. While most citizens lived their whole life in the same neighborhood, the Arridys moved around—having at least eight different addresses. Neither Henry nor Mary finalized their American citizenship, and language remained a problem. According to the 1920 U.S. Census, Mary still did not read or write English. Henry did somewhat better, claiming he could read the new language but not write it. The proper spelling of the family's last name remained fluid—ranging from *Arredy* to *Arraddy* to *Arridy* to *Arrdy*, and back to *Arridy*. As mentioned earlier, Henry must have been unsure of his exact age, and that also was true of Mary. The ages they gave to interviewers varied by as much as six years. Many who came in contact with them never even knew they were Syrian. They often were characterized as Mexican or Italian.

Other bewilderments that struck the family may have left them even more unsettled in their New World existence. A daughter, Amelia, who was born on February 8, 1919, died one year and ten days later.

In 1921, six-year-old Joe began his education at Bessemer Elementary School. In 1922, shortly after the beginning of his second year, the principal called on the Arridy family. She told the parents that Joe could not learn and asked them to keep him at home. The parents reported that for the next four years, Joe merely stayed around the house. They said he was always a passive but happy child. He was the happiest when he was alone, playing all by himself. His favorite pastime was making mud pies.

Today there are communities in America where people would value and support the Arridy family. There are pastors, advocates, helping professionals, and just plain good neighbors who—according to an evolving standard of decency—could see that they had gifts and weaknesses, just like the rest of us. Those people would emphasize their competencies and gifts, and help them compensate for their weaknesses so well that they would not be seen as different and strange.

One thing is sure: Today, no public school would dare tell parents to just keep their child at home. By law, the school would need to come up with some good alternatives.

But there must have been many caring people in those days who did support the Arridys from time to time, or they never would have hung on as well as they did.

6

DIVERSITY'S DARK SIDE

Our country's history is filled with stories describing amazing advancements that came about when people with differences came together, adjusted to one another, and created a culture together. But when certain diverse groups did reach a plateau together, they marveled at their advancements—and then seemed to get stuck. They became fearful of losing all they had gained when wave after wave of immigrants caused "strangers" to appear on the scene. After all, these new people brought with them their own religions, folk ways, national foods, and not least, their own national fears and prejudices.

This frightened the earlier cross-cultural-creating Americans. They came to the irrational conclusion that these newcomers were mentally deficient. They became so fearful that they simply could not tell the difference between those with unfamiliar cultural habits that needed to be understood, and those with mental disabilities who needed special help! In their minds, all these strange and different ones needed to be stopped before they destroyed all the rich gains that "Americans" had achieved. This panic unleashed a Pandora's box of prejudices that today we are still trying to overcome.

By 1900, sudden surges of immigrants were coming from countries east of Germany—Hungary, Poland, Russia. The earlier Germans viewed them as lower-bred "slavs"—broad-headed, shorter, barrel-chested, brown-eyed, brown-haired, and less intelligent. New floods of humanity also arrived from countries surrounding the Mediterranean Sea—people stereotyped as even shorter and darker and dumber—people from Turkey, Greece, southern Italy, and even little Syria.

This new flood of "foreigners" was met with a counterflood of frenzied writings by many of the country's first intellectuals—Nordics (northwestern Europeans) with Anglo-Saxon surnames and Ivy League degrees.

Francis A. Walker, president of the Massachusetts Institute of Technology, sounded one of the first alarms in the June, 1896, *Atlantic Monthly*. He lamented that half the foreigners now entering our ports were "Hungarians, Bohemians, Poles, south Italians and Russian Jews." He characterized them as an "ignorant and brutalized peasantry . . . beaten men from beaten races, representing the worst failures in the struggle for existence."

Another professor at M.I.T., William Z. Ripley, divided all Europeans into three distinct types—Nordics, Alpines, and Mediterraneans (1899). Using Ripley's tripartite divisions, Frederick A. Woods claimed that Mediterraneans were responsible for all labor disputes, because "all the Nordic peoples have an instinctive horror of anything other than well-organized government" (1906).

Harvard professor Prescott Farnsworth Hall, one of the founding leaders of the Immigration Restriction League, unleashed countless press releases to newspapers across the land, claiming that the immigrant outpouring from southern and eastern Europe was "degrading the American character." The IRL became so powerful that a lobbying office was set up in Washington, D.C., with famous Boston Brahmin Senator Henry Cabot Lodge serving as spokesman (Torrey, 1992, pp. 44-45).

Charles B. Davenport, a geneticist from Harvard and a leader in the IRL, believed that all personality characteristics are inherited, including such traits as nomadism, prostitution, pauperism, and an inborn love of the sea (which he believed was a sex-linked recessive gene and therefore found only in males). A zealous eugenist, Davenport believed that the most urgent need of humankind was to "annihilate the hideous serpent of hopelessly vicious protoplasm" (Torrey, 1992, p. 43).

❏ ❏ ❏

In 1915, the year of Joe Arridy's birth, a wiry little man with shiny coal-black hair and mustache became president of the American Association for the Study of the Feebleminded (known today as the American Association on Mental Retardation). His name was Henry Herbert Goddard, and in spite of his Nordic background, he was the spitting image of a wiry little Syrian named Henry Arridy—the same physical build, the same type of mustache and color of hair. Even their hairlines receded in the same fashion.

Earlier, Goddard became captivated by Gregor Mendel's experiments in growing pea plants. Mendel believed that a single recessive gene caused some plants to be dwarfed, with peas that were wrinkled and puny. Mendel believed that if he could breed out that one recessive gene, the plants would become tall and robust. From this, Goddard played with the idea that human beings—like peas—might carry a single recessive gene that could render them irrevocably "feebleminded."

Goddard then studied a test developed in 1905 by Alfred Binet, a French educator who merely had tried to predict which children would do well in French schools, no more and no less. And though Binet pleaded long and loudly that his test never should be used for measuring intelligence, Goddard chose to do exactly that (Gould, 1981, pp. 155-57).

Goddard identified a family lineage, and then evaluated all the ancestors who were still alive. After analyzing his data, he did indeed claim that feeblemindedness obeyed the Mendelian rules of inheritance. To make his point for all the world to see, he wrote *The Kallikak Family* (1912). In that book, Goddard told the amazing story of Martin Kallikak, Sr., a noble Revolutionary soldier of "good English blood" who, at a tavern frequented by the militia during the war, met and slept with a "feebleminded" woman. By this woman, he became the father of a "feebleminded" son. Although Martin, Sr., was long gone at the time of the birth, the woman, in a not-so-feebleminded way, named her son Martin Kallikak, Jr. After the war, Kallikak, Sr., returns home and marries a more respectable woman.

Goddard traced and charted the two lineages of offspring started by Kallikak, Sr.—one that began with his wartime peccadillo and one that emanated from his respectable marriage:

> The foregoing charts and text tell a story as instructive as it is amazing. We have here a family of good English blood of the middle class, settling upon the original land purchased from the proprietors of the state in Colonial times, and throughout four generations maintaining a reputation for honor and respectability of which they are justly proud. Then a scion of this family, in an unguarded moment, steps aside from the paths of rectitude and with the help of a feebleminded girl, starts a line of mental defectives that is truly appalling. After this mistake, he returns to the traditions of his family, marries a woman of his own quality, and through her carries on a line of respectability equal to that of his ancestors.
>
> *We thus have two series from two different mothers but the same father.* These extend for six generations. Both lines live out their lives in practically the same region and in the same environment (p. 50).

Goddard claimed to have identified 480 descendants caused by sexual intercourse with the "feebleminded woman," of whom many were also "feebleminded," as well as illegitimate, sexually immoral, and alcoholic. There were prostitutes, epileptics, criminals, paupers, perverts, welfare clients, whorehouse madams, horse thieves, and one was even "of the Mongolian type."

On the other hand, Goddard traced the lineage from the upper-crust marriage:

> Martin Sr., on leaving the Revolutionary army, straightened up and married a respectable girl of good family, and through that union has come another line of descendants of radically different character. These now number four hundred and ninety-six in direct descent. All of them are normal people. Three men only have been found among them who were somewhat degenerate, but they were not defective. Two of these were alcoholic, and the other sexually loose.
>
> All of the legitimate children of Martin Sr. married into the best families of their states, the descendants of colonial governors, signers of the Declaration of Independence, soldiers and even the founders of a great university. Indeed, in this family and its collateral branches, we find nothing but good representative citizenship. There are doctors, lawyers, judges, educators, traders, landholders; in short, respectable citizens, men and women prominent in every phase of social life (pp. 29-30).

Then Goddard issued his big scare for the whole nation to swallow:

> There are Kallikak families all about us. They are multiplying at twice the rate of the general population, and not until we recognize this fact, and work on this basis, will we begin to solve these social problems (p. 70).

And with this scare, he gave the world a new word—*moron*. Morons were people with feeblemindedness who functioned the highest. Since they often passed for normal, they were the most dangerous, the most despicable of all. The only way to find these persons with diseased germ plasm was to give them intelligence tests and lock them away. Today the term *moron* is used often in the English language, but most don't know that the father of that word was Henry Goddard.

Goddard's proclamations had a powerful effect upon the United Stated Public Health Service. Immediately after the *The Kallikak Family* was published, the USPHS invited Goddard to Ellis Island to apply his mental tests to arriving immigrants. Goddard and his assistants accepted the invitation and went right to work. Shortly afterward, he reported that based upon his examination of the "great mass of average immigrants," 83 percent of the eastern European Jews, 80 percent of Hungarians, 79 percent of Italians, and 87 percent of Russians were "feebleminded" (1913).

In 1914, *Die Familie Kallikak* was published in Germany. In 1933, it was republished after the Nazis came to power.

The name *Kallikak* was actually a pseudonym. The real surname became a closely guarded secret; many scholars set out to discover the real name, but they all failed. Then a young psychology professor, J. David Smith, became a dogged detective who simply would not give up until he broke the code. He looked up many of the members of the family himself. He also interviewed many who recalled certain Kallikaks who had died. He spent days poring over old records in countless courthouses, archives, and libraries. Then in his book *Minds Made Feeble* (1985), he showed that Goddard's pedigree studies were fraudulent. He found that many of the Kallikaks on the supposed "bad side" had been well-liked, productive workers, solid citizens, even community leaders. Many of these people simply did not fit the demeaning descriptions that Goddard had assigned to them.

Stephen Jay Gould, in *The Mismeasure of Man* (1981, pp. 158-74), analyzed the step-by-step logic of Goddard and exposed much of it as being utterly silly. He faulted him for the blatant misuse of Binet's schoolchild test. He challenged Goddard's idea that the remarkable many-faceted aspects of any person's intelligence could be defined by a single number on a single unitary scale. Gould even discovered that photos of the "bad" Kallikaks in Goddard's book had been touched up to make the subjects look more despicable and uglier than they really were!

Goddard's science was laced with what scientist and epidemiologist Ernst Wynder identified as *wish bias*. An investigator can become so hungry to publish positive results that he lifts from his data only that which supports his "wish" and ignores all data that does not. Wynder warns: "A careful review of *all* the evidence, both data that fit and those that do not fit our view, will help both scientific integrity as well as the public, who must react to our findings and messages" (Wynder et al., 1990).

Unfortunately, others took the message of Goddard and ran with it, without testing for the wish bias in his science. Madison Grant, a proud man of Nordic descent and a graduate of Yale, was so moved by it that he produced a book which quickly became the bible of the eugenic movement. In *Passing of the Great Race* (1916), he claimed that Nordics were truly superior and lashed out at all the "wretched outcasts" who passed through Ellis Island—especially "that half-asiatic welter of people we call Russians," and toward Jews in particular. He believed that the qualities of "the Polish Jew—dwarf stature, peculiar mentality and ruthless concentration of self-interest—are being engrafted upon the stock of the nation."

Grant, like Goddard, claimed that the evil genetic protoplasm in a person was more powerful than the good. Therefore, "the cross between a white man and an Indian is an Indian; the cross between a white man and a Negro is a Negro; the cross between the white man and a Hindu is a Hindu; and the cross between any of the three European races and a Jew is a Jew." Grant also made the grand claim that all major contributions to civilization had come from people of Nordic descent, and he claimed also to be able to prove that Jesus Christ had been Nordic (Torrey, p. 43).

The Goddard message gathered force. It attempted to pit race against race and neighbor against neighbor, because more than half of us in America purportedly possessed a terrible, rotten, overpowering gene that could bring us all down. As a result, many Americans began pointing at others as if they were racial and intellectual Typhoid Marys. According to Goddard, those with a rotten gene needed to be singled out. They needed to be culled and colonized. They ought to be sterilized. Others felt that without a doubt, they should be killed.

And so Goddard, who became president of the American Association for the Study of the Feebleminded in the same year Arridy was born, used his Nordic scholarship and Nordic sense of superiority to point an unsympathetic finger at numerous people unlike himself. Some were "foreign" strangers. Others were labeled "feebleminded." It didn't matter.

That finger pointed at a truly likeable Joe Arridy. In another time, with proper understanding and support, he could have achieved a highly valued social role in his society. But due to Goddard's research, Joe possessed two descriptions that shone out to others as if they were neon signs—*Syrian* and *feebleminded*. They shone so brightly that those around him were blinded to the myriad gifts and competencies that could have been discovered in this man.

7

THE HANSEL

The American Dream of 1922 contained no provisions such as we have in our society today for subsidies, community programs, and family supports for children like Joe Arridy. And although Joe was a self-satisfied loner, his expulsion from school that year added to the burden of his family. Then came two more births—George in 1923 and a second Amelia in 1924.

Henry's small laborer's salary now failed to stretch far enough and, with some panic, he sought help from friends, churches, and government officials. Finally, these forces outside the family fingered Joe as the family's central problem, the one who—as in the story of Hansel and Gretel—had to be ditched. Henry was encouraged to contact the Pueblo County Court, which then contacted the Colorado State Home and Training School for Mental Defectives at Grand Junction. Letters regarding Joe and his family's situation flowed back and forth between the two agencies. After being torn between his own feelings for his son and what others told him he should do, Henry finally signed court documents as "the person making the complaint." A hearing before a lunacy commission of two doctors was held. Then, on October 30, 1925, in *Peoples Case No. 16598,* Judge Frank G. Mirick handed down his decision and pounded his gavel:

> It is therefore ordered that the said Joe Arridy be committed to the State Home and Training School for Mental Defectives, to be detained and trained therein as the law directs and that the Sheriff of Pueblo County is hereby designated as the person to accompany said person to said State Home and Training School for Mental Defectives.
>
> We therefore command you, the said Sheriff of Pueblo County, to deliver with all convenient speed, the said Joe Arridy to the superintendent of said State Home and Training School for Mental Defectives, together with a copy hereof as his warrant, to be by said superintendent safely kept and cared for until discharged according to law.

These were strong-sounding words for such a meek guy. Little did anyone know that Joe would be forced to stand and hear similar judgments in the years to come. All would be crafted to remove him from society, and even from the world.

On November 2, the deputy clerk of the county court wrote to Dr. Carl W. Plumb, the superintendent of the institution at Grand Junction:

Dear Doctor:

This letter will introduce Henry Arridy, the father of Joe Arridy, who has kindly consented to bring his son to the school and pay all expenses of the trip. He is a little hard to get everything through his head but understands that Joe is to remain in the school until you see fit to release him.

I rather think that with careful attention, the boy will improve. The mother's mentality is not of the highest and the family consists of several other living children besides several who died at childbirth.

The father has his hands full trying to care for the mother and children but is willing to buy clothes for Joe from time to time. He has nothing but his daily wages and his expenses are heavy.

One of the examining board was at one time family physician and knew Joe's condition thoroughly.

Respectfully,
C. V. Crouse, Deputy Clerk

On November 3, Henry Arridy somehow transported his son from Pueblo on the eastern slope of the Rocky Mountains, through 287 miles of winding canyons and passes to Grand Junction on the western slope. He left his son at the school for mental defectives. He must have known that the distance between Pueblo and Grand Junction made it almost impossible to get together with his son as long as he stayed at the institution.

❏ ❏ ❏

Joe was received by Helen D. Cover, R.N., the institution's matron. Judging from her correspondence, she like Joe and cared about what happened to him.

According to the rules of the institution, Joe was isolated for "examination and observation" for the first ten days. During that time, he was given The Stanford Revision of the Binet-Simon Tests (Terman, 1916). The 12-page test booklet, stapled in his institutional records, showed that a tester named L. Hopkirk made notations on the simplest functions in only the first two and a half pages. According to Hopkirk, Joe could point to his nose, eyes, mouth, and hair. He identified a key, a penny, a closed knife, a watch, and a pencil. He gave his name and sex. He repeated correctly sentences with up to seven syllables ("I have a dog." "The dog runs after the cat." "In summer the sun is hot."). He copied a square and a diamond with a pencil. He counted four pennies.

Then the test began to get tough. Joe failed, "What must you do when you are sleepy?" (His answer: "eat.") "What must you do when you are cold?" was scored a partial because Joe said, "Go inside." The correct answer was, "Put on a coat."

He flunked the repeating of four digits (4-7-3-9 got no response; 2-8-5-4 got 8-4-5; 7-2-6-1 received no answer). When he was shown the color red, he said it was black. Yellow was correctly called yellow, blue was called red, and green was described as blue. He gave his age as nine when he was really ten.

He just sat silently when he was asked to tell the difference between a fly and butterfly, a stone and an egg, as well as wood and glass. He also sat silently when he was asked to name the days of the week. He didn't even try. A later notation showed in his records that most of his sentences were incomplete, containing only two or three words.

Hopkirk computed Joe's score and gave him an Intelligence Quotient of 46 (a dead-center normal person was supposed to have an IQ of 100). According to Hopkirk, Joe's intelligence was the same as that of a four-year-and-ten month-old child. Hopkirk found Joe to be totally passive. Never did he initiate or make a move on his own. He only tried to respond to the leading of the examiner. Hopkirk wrote that Joe Arridy was *an imbecile*.

❏ ❏ ❏

An admission questionnaire from the Pueblo court arrived in Grand Junction and was placed in Joe's institutional record. The deputy clerk, C. V. Crouse, had written down the oral responses of Henry and Mary Arridy. Although many questions remained unanswered, many that were responded to stood out:

Does the child talk? (Somewhat)
At what age did it begin to talk? (5 years)
Is the child inclined to run away? (Yes)
Does the child realize the difference between right and wrong? (Somewhat)
State any preference for food? (Grapes)
Is the child nervous (No)
Does it come when called (Yes, sometimes)
Is it good tempered or otherwise? (Good natured)
Is it abusive to other children? (Seems to be afraid of other children and is jealous)
What kind of punishment has been resorted to? (None)
Has the child manifested any mechanical talent? (Likes to hammer nails)
Was it ever in public school? If so, how long? (Two years)
Can the child add? (No); Subtract (No); Read? (No); Write? (No); Recognize color? (No);
    Sing? (No)
Can it do an errand? (Sometimes will do a simple errand.)
What kind of work can the child do? (None)
Is it fond of children? (Is afraid of children)
Is it fond of play (Likes to play by himself, makes mud pies, etc.)
Does it hide, break or destroy things? (Yes)
How does it amuse itself? (Plays like a two-year-old child)

The father signed *Henry Arrdy*, and the mother merely made her mark, with Crouse the clerk signing as a witness.

A medical doctor, J. L. McGonigle, found Joe to be in good physical health, but when he learned that Henry and Mary Arridy were first cousins, he made a notation. He also noted that the family had contained six children, of which three were dead. One of the dead children was never identified in any of the records.

After ten days, Joe became a regular resident of the institution. It was comprised of six buildings—an administration building, a combination school and auditorium, a hospital, a main dining room, and kitchen, as well as a girls' building and a boys' building. According to the institution's Sixth Biennial Report (1931), approximately 266 inmates lived there. All were indelibly labeled and neatly classified (64 idiots, 131 imbeciles, 71 morons).

Joe was placed with 73 other boys in a ward containing an equal number of beds in one room, and a large day room with about the same amount of chairs. Life for the most part was based on common-denominator rules: Everyone went to bed at the same time, spent most of their daylight hours in the day room, and were herded together to the dining hall three times a day. The attendants—two to three during the day and one at night—prided themselves on their ability to keep the inmates under control. The attendants could have been the kindest people in their own families and neighborhoods. At the institution, however, with all the children in their charge, they were forced to function like army sergeants. Much of their time was spent setting limits ("Sam, stop hitting Bill, or I'll put you in the seclusion room." "No, Tom, I can't let you do that, because if I did, I'd have to let all the kids do it."). At other times, they functioned like cattle drovers ("Come on, boys, head 'em up, move 'em out. It's time to go to the dining room"). Sixty-five patients throughout the institution were allowed to break away from the regimented life to attend school for three hours a day. The first hour was for reading and writing. Then the girls moved into needle work, garment making, rug weaving, and basketry, while the boys worked on fibre-reed furniture, made brushes, made wood furniture, and also did rug weaving and basketry.

Joe was not in that group. And he was too small to be in the group of boys who cared for five horses, 20 milk cows, one bull and one heifer—or fed 30 stock hogs, 100 shoats, 16 brood sows, and one hard-working boar. Nor did he help with the daily feeding of 300 old hens and 600 young chickens.

He did, however, attend some of the group "entertainments": picnics, a weekly motion picture, and holiday celebrations. When the circus came to town, everyone who was physically able marched in formation to an afternoon matinee. Some of the older boys, however, did not march back, causing the sheriff to stop the departing circus train just outside of town. He removed all the patients who had planned to run away with the circus and delivered them back to the institution.

A "good patient" was one who remained reasonably healthy and pleasant, and did not break any of the ward's commonly held rules. When an inmate was caught in a transgression, that breech of rules was written up and placed in the inmate's record. A problem inmate usually acquired a thick institutional record filled with "critical incident reports," while a good patient's record remained comparatively thin. Shy, quiet Joe was a good patient. He stayed by himself. He didn't make waves. His record during this time period was spotlessly clean.

But his first stay at the institution was short.

8

ANGUISHING FATHER

Joe Arridy was gone, but his father's misery remained. He missed his son. Then, being the indecisive worry wart that he was, he began to ask others if he had done the right thing. Finally, he came to the conclusion that he wanted Joe to come home. On July 24, 1926—just nine months after Joe's admission to the institution—Henry got a friend to type the following letter:

Dr. Carl W. Plumb, Supt.
State Home for Mental Defectives
Grand Junction, Colorado

Dear Sir:

I am writing you in regard to my son, Joe Arridy, who was committed to your institution October 30, 1925.

About October 1st, I am planning on moving to Detroit, Michigan, and would like very much to take my son with me. I intend placing him in a school in Detroit if you will let me have him.

If it is satisfactory with you, I shall come after him about the 25th of August.

Hoping that it can be arranged to let me have my son, I am,

Very truly yours,

Henry Arridy
1708 Pine Street
Pueblo, Colorado

On August 5, Superintendent Plumb wrote a letter in response: "If you want to take your son, Joe, from this institution, I would suggest that you talk to your County Judge: explain the situation to him and ask him for a release. If he grants the release, you may come for the boy at any time, and I will be glad to let you have him."

Although no written release was found, Henry must have received a go-ahead from someone. On August 13, he arrived at the institution and met with Plumb, who then scrawled an impromptu release on a sheet of the institution's letterhead:

August 13, 1926.

On the above date I received from Dr. C. W. Plumb, Supt, Joe Arridy for whom I assume the entire responsibility.

Henry Arridy signed at the bottom of the page. He took his son back to Pueblo. The family did not move to Detroit.

9

THE OUTRAGED OFFICIAL

Home again and now age 11, Joe Arridy returned to his childish self-amusements—but not for long. He soon gave up mud-pie making for long walks. He could be seen walking all over town, his legs stretching for long strides, his arms swinging in wide arcs and his eyes seemingly fixed on destinations that appeared to be miles ahead. Even so, he remained passive and shy with others. He bothered nobody. He just kept moving. There were times, however, when others chose to cross his path and bother him.

As time passed, the family did less and less to restrict Joe's wanderings. Part of the reason probably stemmed from Henry's transition from the iron works to bootlegging. At that time, Prohibition was the law of the land, even though the drinking of wine, beer, and other alcoholic beverages was a valued tradition in the cultures of many recent immigrants—especially the Irish, Italians, Jews, and Poles (Clark, 1976). So Henry saw a chance to make better money. But he wasn't very slick at the job, and jail sentences often kept him away from his home. As for Mary, she always seemed at a loss about how to deal with her son. The pity of it all was that, in those days, there weren't any professional or volunteer agencies willing to help sustain, guide, and support parents with a child like Joe. No special education in the public schools. No day programs. No parental counseling. No support services. No understanding and committed citizen advocates and friends.

On September 17, 1929, when Joe was 14, his roving came to a sudden halt. On that day, a probation officer picked up the boy in the morning and mailed a hurriedly typed letter in the afternoon. The letter was addressed to Superintendent Plumb at the institution in Grand Junction:

Peoples Case No. 16598 [The case number of Judge Mirick's earlier commitment]
IN RE: Joseph Arridy, A Mental Defective
Dear Doctor:
    Referring to the above case, this boy was committed to the State Home and Training School at Grand Junction on October 30, 1925 and was delivered there November 3rd, 1925. He was some time thereafter released to his father and brought back to Pueblo. He is one of the worst Mental Defective cases that I have ever seen, he cannot read or write and is not allowed to go to school for the reason he does not accomplish any thing. I picked him up this morning for allowing some of the nastiest and Dirtiest things done to him that I have ever heard of. It is so dirty that I can not mention it in the letter but will slip it to you on the side. The County Commissioners will not pay the expenses of returning this boy as they say that he was sent

there, at one time at the expense of the County and they will not pay for the return, as it is up to the Institution, after being paroled by them. The boy MUST be returned. The people of the neighborhood are indignant as they are afraid of the boy and think that he never should have been turned loose. I do not in any way mean to criticize the actions of the Institution but I can not understand why boys of the mentality of this one are allowed to return home. Some day one of these boys is going to commit some crime that will be some what like the Hickman case. It has always been my understanding that when a boy or girl is committed to one of these institutions he is kept there for all time and that the Superintendent has not the power to parole them. I may be wrong in this and if I am I would appreciate it if you will refer me to the Section of the law that permits it. I wish that you would wire me, on receipt of this letter advising what I shall do with this boy. Will you send for him or shall I have him returned. The boy is in Woodcroft Hospital. With kind regards, I am,
Yours very truly,
[Signature]

The things that were too dirty to mention in the letter were typed up on a half-page sheet and stapled to the letter:

CRIME AGAINST NATURE, manipulating the Penis' of Negro Boys with his mouth.
SODOMY, Allowing "Nigger" Boys to Enter the "Dirty Road" with their Penis.
Sleeps with "Nigger" boys at their homes and what goes on is not known.
His father and mother know these things and have known them. His father, Henry Arridy is in jail at this time on a charge of Boot-Legging.
[Signature]
(I would be more technical but do not know the terms)

The official's use of the term *allowing* was key to understanding Joe. Time and time again one found statements showing how others beat Joe and used him. Because of the way he was, and because others were so prejudiced, so misunderstanding, and so cruel to people like him in those days, he was always a target. Never, in all the records, could one find a single instance in which Joe was even physically assertive. As for his ever being aggressive, he just didn't have it in him. Joe was vulnerable. And in those early days of the robust thrusting forward after the higher plateaus of the American Dream, Joe's laid-back personality made him despicable in the eyes of others.

Today a probation officer might have sensed Joe's situation and moved more slowly and carefully. He might have taken Joe into custody, but he would have sought help from other resources within the community.

Joe's probation officer, however, hadn't even dreamed of such options. He saw him as a "mental deficient." He saw him as disgusting, and he cast him out. He was only intent upon cleansing his district, as the eugenicists had preached.

Lewis M. Terman, the psychologist who developed the test that was given to Joe Arridy, went on to believe that intelligence testing was the one great hope for society. He later argued that "If all people could be tested, and then sorted into roles appropriate for their intelligence, then a just, and, above all, efficient society might be constructed for the first time in history" (Gould, p. 180). Then Terman expanded from mere testing to the consideration of racial backgrounds. This move was evident when he discussed laboring men and servant girls:

> The tests have told the truth. . . . No amount of school instruction will ever make them intelligent voters or capable citizens. . . . They represent the level of intelligence which is very, very common among Spanish-Indian and Mexican families of the Southwest and also among negroes. Their dullness seems to be racial, or at least inherent in the family stocks from which they came. . . . There is no possibility at present of convincing society that they should not be allowed to reproduce, although from a eugenic point of view they constitute a grave problem because of their unusually prolific breeding (Terman, 1916, pp. 91-92).

Charles Davenport's influence gathered force after he became the first director of a powerful agency called the Eugenics Records Office. He defined eugenics as the "science of the improvement of the human race by better breeding" (1911, p. 1). The purpose of the records office: "[The] accumulation and study of records of physical and mental characteristics of human families, to the end that people may be better advised as to fit and unfit marriages" (Crissey, 1983, p. 60). Davenport was instrumental in setting up "Fitter Families" contests at state fairs, with awards given to "Grade A Individuals." Protestant churches sponsored a eugenic sermon contest, in which Davenport helped select the winning entry (Torrey, p. 44).

In 1917, Harvard professor Robert M. Yerkes organized the intelligence testing of draftees being inducted for World War I, and if one wants to gain a clear picture of the mindboggling mixups of this venture, they need only read Stephen Jay Gould's *The Mismeasure of Man* (pp. 192-233). After the war, Yerkes reported that the average white American possessed a mental age of what a person should possess at 13.08 years of age. A few years earlier, Terman had claimed it to be 16 years. To the average worker in the eugenic scare movement, this difference supported their prediction that those with the rotten genes were indeed dragging the rest of the population down—rapidly. Yerkes found also that the average Russian American possessed the mental age of 11.34 years; the Italian American, 11.01; the Polish American, 10.74 years. The African American was claimed by Yerkes to have a mental age of 10.41 years (Yerkes, 1921, p. 742). With scores like these, Yerkes felt that Nordic supremacy was not a jingoistic prejudice.

In 1923, Carl C. Brigham of Princeton published *A Study of American Intelligence,* as an attempt to translate the Army test data into social action. This small but powerful book began with an introduction by Yerkes, who praised Brigham for his objectivity. Then Brigham used the Army data to amplify and add to what Grant had said seven years earlier, in *The Passing of the Great Race:* He epitomizes the Nordics as the very best human beings on the face of the earth. Then he takes the usual whacks at Alpines and Mediterraneans. He added some of his own touches, however, when he said that Nordics were usually "domineering, individualistic, self-reliant . . . and as a result they are usually Protestants." Alpines, on the other hand, are "submissive to authority both political and religious, being usually Roman Catholics . . . the perfect slave, the ideal serf, the model subject" (pp. 182-83).

The Army data and Brigham's book served as springboards for convincing the U.S. Congress to vote the Immigration Restriction Act of 1924. This act set the annual quota of immigrants at 2 percent of the population of citizens who had already arrived from each country. That sounded fair enough—until one found that these deft politicians based their 2 percent quotas on the 1890 census, rather than the one conducted in 1920. In 1890, most citizens were still Nordic. And so the door remained wide open to them. But the door to other countries was barely cracked. When President Calvin Coolidge signed the bill, he stated emphatically that "America must be kept American."

In an interesting sidelight, the U.S. Army fliers involved in "The Great [Around-the-World] Air Race of 1924" landed in Tokyo just as Coolidge signed the Immigration Restriction Act. The fliers found the Japanese devastated by the American law. At first they couldn't believe that the U.S. could do such a thing—the country that just one year earlier had so kindly and thoughtfully loaned the people of Tokyo $150 million to help them recover from the worst earthquake in history, one that leveled Tokyo and killed 140,000 people. The warmth they felt suddenly dissolved into protests and demonstrations against America, for what they labeled "the Japanese exclusion act." Although the Japanese treated the American fliers with warmth and deep respect, the fliers were continually aware of the pain the U.S. had caused. For example, Lt. Lowell Smith, who became friendly with a Japanese flight officer, related that one night at dinner, Smith's host said, "You know, I like you. I like everything about the United States, but someday we fight" (WGBH/TV, 1989).

After the eugenicist victory in the congress, Carl Brigham became secretary of the College Entrance Examination Board, where he devised and developed the Scholastic Aptitude Test (Kamin, 1976, p. 379).

After the near lockout of foreigners with "bad blood," the eugenicists moved to mop up within the country. Goddard argued that anyone who threatened the better "human stock" should be segregated and prevented from reproduction (Smith, 1985, p. 137). Consequently, every state began to build institutions and put people in them.

Harry Laughlin, an energetic leader at the Eugenic Records Office, became fiercely committed to the development of state laws requiring sterilization of all persons believed to be hereditary defectives. According to David Smith, he included "tramps, beggars, alcoholics, criminals, the feebleminded, the insane, epileptics, the physically deformed, the blind, and the deaf. It is interesting to note that Laughlin himself was epileptic" (p. 138).

In 1924, Laughlin developed a model sterilization law for the state of Virginia. In that same year, Carrie Buck, age 17, became pregnant from what she claimed was rape. Her foster parents had her admitted to the Virginia Colony for Epileptics and the Feebleminded. Her mother, Emma Buck, had been admitted three years earlier to the same institution. After Carrie gave birth to a daughter, Doris, Laughlin knew that he had the subject for his test case. He lobbied the legislature to enact state legislation to sterilize certain inmates of Virginia institutions—including Carrie Buck. The case wound its way up to the U.S. Supreme Court in 1927, and under pressure from Laughlin and his colleagues, the court upheld Virginia's sterilization law.

Oliver Wendell Holmes, in *Buck v Bell*, wrote the opinion that the eugenicists amplified throughout the land in their speeches and literature, especially the following passage:

We have seen more than once that the public welfare may call upon the best citizens for their lives. It would be strange if it could not call upon those who already sap the strength of the state for these lesser sacrifices, often not felt to be such by those concerned, in order to prevent our being swamped with incompetence. It is better for all the world, if instead of waiting to execute degenerate offspring for crime, or let them starve for their imbecility, society can prevent those who are manifestly unfit from continuing their kind . . . . Three generations of imbeciles are enough.

Strong words. It set off 4,000 sterilizations in Virginia, more than 50,000 nationally, and better than 56,000 in Germany. But later experts tracked down Carrie Buck Detamore and Doris Buck Figgins. They found them living reasonably happy and so-called normal lives. Investigating further, they concluded that neither Carrie, nor her mother, nor her daughter had any mental retardation or illness at all (Smith, 1985, pp. 150-55).

In 1927, the same year Oliver Wendell Holmes rendered his opinion, Adolph Hitler published *Mein Kampf* [My Struggle]. And in it he stated, "The right of personal freedom recedes before the duty to preserve the race. The demand that defective people be prevented from propagating equally defective offspring is a demand of clearest reason and if systematically executed represents the most humane act of mankind" (p. 255).

Later, in 1936, Harry Laughlin received a Hitler-inspired honorary medical doctor's degree from the University at Heidelberg, Germany. The degree was conferred in appreciation for his services to the science of eugenics and his efforts to purify "the human seed stock" (Smith, p. 157). Then on September 17, 1929, with the Nordics frantically grasping for "the purity" of great America, it is understandable that the probation officer could be so outraged by an "allowing" Joe Arridy, an "imbecile," a Syrian-American, a Roman Catholic caught in an indiscretion with African Americans.

10

ANGUISHING
FATHER—AGAIN

When Henry Arridy got out of jail and discovered that Joe was in Grand Junction, he began another campaign to get his son back. He contacted many authorities, but the incident that had provoked Joe's removal was still fresh in their minds. Over time, however, the power people began to mellow. But Henry did not.

After Dr. Plumb died, Dr. Benjamin L. Jefferson, a medical doctor, became superintendent, and Henry traveled to Grand Junction to try to talk the new superintendent into letting his son go. Although Jefferson probably did not as yet know Joe very well, he undoubtedly consulted his records. If he did, I'm sure that the correspondence from the 1929 incident screamed at him to keep the boy in the institution.

Henry hounded the principal of Bessemer School, until on April 13, 1932, she wrote to the superintendent for reinforcement:

Superintendent Weak-minded Institution
Dear Sir:
   I am writing at the request of Joe Arrdy's father in regard to Joe. His father has the idea that Joe can be cured by medicine and will soon be able to come home.
   I have tried to explain to him that Joe is better off in the school but he insists that Joe was promised that he could come home about this time.
   Will you kindly write and make it plain that the boy must stay at the school?
   We had him in this school for three or four years [other records state less than two years] so we know his condition.
   I am sorry to bother you with the request to write but Mr. Arrdy was so insistent that I finally promised him I would write to inquire about Joe.
Very truly yours,
Linah Swanzey, Principal

Dr. Jefferson responded on April 20.

Dear Miss Swanzey:
   I have your letter of April 13th in which you refer to Joe Arridy's father and inquire for Joe's possible release.
   When Mr. Arridy visited me some time ago, I explained to him the perverse habits of Joe which it would not be possible for me to permit him to leave the institution. You may advise

him accordingly and reiterate to Mr. Arridy that it will not be possible for me to, under the circumstances, permit Joe to leave the institution. Also please advise him that we are taking special pains to help Joe in every way possible. I shall be pleased to have his father and mother visit him whenever they find it convenient to do so.
Very truly yours,
B. F. Jefferson, Superintendent

The perverse habit Dr. Jefferson mentioned may have included passive fellatio or sodomy, as discovered by the probation officer. But Dr. Jefferson often made it plain that the number-one perverse habit in his institution was masturbation. According to his many notes and statements, masturbation was the chief scourge. It was seen by him as the terrible precursor to all the rest. Many inmates probably responded to Jefferson's campaign to stamp out this "scourge" by doing it furtively and in private. Joe may not have been as discreet. It was fortunate, however, that Joe was not a resident at the institution in a nearby state. In the Winfield, Kansas, State Training School, the prescribed treatment for such an act was castration (Trent, 1994, pp. 120, 195; Wood, 1951, pp. 3-4).

Henry then worked on the clerk of the Pueblo County Court until he sent a letter to Dr. Jefferson on July 21, 1933:

Dear Sir:
I am writing in behalf of Mr. Henry Arridy, who was in the office today in regard to his son Joe, an inmate of the Home.
Mr. Arridy would like to know if you think Joe's condition is such that it would be advisable to parole him to his father. If so, Mr. Arridy will come for the boy.
Very truly yours,
L. T. Morgan, Clerk
PS: Please send me a few application blanks. Can you accept any boys or girls at this time?

Dr. Jefferson replied on July 31.

Dear Mr. Morgan:
I have your letter in reference to Joe Arridy.
Am sorry to say that Joe, while not as much as heretofore did, still practices his perverse habits, therefore, I cannot recommend his parole and feel that it would be better to keep him here.
As per your request, we are enclosing application blanks.
Very truly yours,
Dr. B. F. Jefferson, Superintendent

And so Henry Arridy struck out again. Probably nobody in those days gave him much credit for the way he fought for his son. Today, a tenacious and energetic father like Henry could have captured the attention of many who are committed to helping the Arridys of the world. Many agencies that now exist in Pueblo would have respected Henry for what he tried to do.

11

STRUCTURE

There are certain colonies of people in the world who have chosen, or have been forced, to live together. When that happens, almost everything a person does is controlled by a single official. A thoughtful sociologist, Erving Goffman, studied such places and found that all of them contained the same basic structure:

First, all aspects of life are conducted in the same place and under the same single authority. Second, each phase of the member's daily activity is carried on in the immediate company of a large batch of others, all of whom are treated alike and required to do the same thing together. Third, all phases of the day's activities are tightly scheduled, with one activity leading at a prearranged time into the next, the whole sequence of activities being imposed from above by a system of explicit formal rulings and a body of officials. Finally, the various enforced activities are brought together into a single rational plan purportedly designed to fulfill the official aims of the institution (1961, p. 6).

Goffman claimed that these characteristics can be found in homes for the aged, sanitariums for persons with tuberculosis, mental hospitals, jails and penitentiaries, prisoner-of-war camps, army barracks, navy ships. They also can be found in boarding schools, abbeys, and convents (pp. 4-5).

The Colorado State Home and Training School for Mental Defectives possessed a structure that most certainly equaled the ones Goffman described:

6:00 A.M.	Everyone gets up and gets dressed before the ward workers' shift change.
7:00	Night workers leave and day workers arrive.
7:00-8:00	Move in ward groups to dining hall according to feeding schedule.
9:00	Assigned activity groups at school, farm, recreation. Those with no activity sit in the day room of their ward.
11:30	Back to ward and get ready for lunch.
12:00 Noon	Move in ward groups to dining hall according to feeding schedule.
1:00 P.M.	Assigned activities or day room sitting.
3:00	Day ward workers leave and evening workers arrive.
4:00	Most day activities cease.
5:00	Move in ward groups to dining hall according to feeding schedule.
Evening	Structured recreational activities or day room sitting.

9:00   Everyone in bed.
11:00   Evening ward workers leave and night workers arrive.

Such a structure ignores for the most part the individual needs and preferences of a person. But Joe, living in an era when there were no solid community services or supports, probably benefited more from the structure of the institution than from his aimless wanderings all over Pueblo.

Joe never was included in the groups that went to the school or the farm. At first he spent most of his waking hours secure and alone on the day ward. Because of his reclusive nature, others tended to tease him, but the ward attendants protected him.

The residents' institution records in those days focused more on lists of the bad things a resident did or experienced, not the successes, the good milestones of growth, as they are recorded today. For example, I recall that a teenager ran away from an institution where I once worked. He was gone for two weeks before returning on his own. When he returned, he described with enthusiasm where he went, what he saw, and how he survived at night. For him, the elopement was a remarkable learning experience. And yet, the only thing recorded in the institutional record was a critical incident report which noted his time of departure and return, and that a nurse applied bacitracin on his sunburned neck. Since the young man wandered off quite frequently, he was never recognized for what he learned in these forays. The many incident reports merely confirmed him as "a runner" who had to be watched.

Once the probation officer's letter was placed in Joe Arridy's file, it would forever damn him as "a pervert." The incident would be recited over the years in clinical conferences, and unfortunately, much of this was included as well in the court records that followed.

Joe's problem: He had yet to learn to masturbate in secret, as the many other inmates did. When he did, staff members assumed that his sexual perversity had improved. One interesting statement in the record points out that Joe never showed any sexual affection for women.

Finally Joe was given a day activity, working in the kitchen. He became close to a Mrs. Bowers, who may have taken a liking to him and reported regularly on his behavior during his working hours. His capabilities: "Tasks of not too long duration; can wash dishes, do mopping of floors, can do small chores and errands. He depends on others for leadership and suggestions."

He may have gotten along better with older people than with his peers. And so he became a regular in the kitchen, right up until the time he made a new discovery that took him away from Grand Junction forever.

12

BOXCARS

One month and seven days after the probation officer demanded the exclusion of Joe Arridy from regular society, the country's economy slipped into a black hole called the Great Depression. It started on Thursday, October 24, 1929. Stocks went into a crash dive. Then came a terrible chain reaction that affected the whole world. World trade declined. Each country tried to save itself by raising tariffs on imported goods. This standoff only made things worse. Countries changed their forms of government. The depression even led to the rise of Adolph Hitler in Germany, and it moved the Japanese to invade China. The Great Depression actually didn't end until the U.S. entered World War II in 1941. One reaction to the depression during those hard times influenced Joe Arridy.

More than 200,000 young people wandered through the country, seeking food, clothing, shelter, and jobs. They traveled by jumping onto railroad freight cars, and when they weren't moving across the nation, they lived in camps called hobo jungles (McElvaine, 1985).

In 1936, residents of the Grand Junction School for Mental Defectives witnessed this amazing movement of people as trains passed near the institution. They saw people—lots of people—sitting on top of box cars, in the open doors of empty cars, or on flat-bed cars. In the freight yards, just north of the institution, no one could be seen on the trains. But as soon as they left the yards and picked up speed, people were seen running alongside, grabbing hold and jumping on.

On a warm Saturday, August 8, 1936, Joe Arridy, now 22, discovered boxcar riding. He and another fellow, a 16-year-old, left work at the kitchen. They were supposed to return to their wards, but instead, they walked off the grounds. They did not return that night. On Sunday morning, Joe's kitchen-working friend jumped a train heading west for Salt Lake City, but Joe did not go.

Later in the day, three more youngsters walked off the grounds, and they saw Joe in the freight yards. The four slept in a boxcar that evening. On Monday morning, the group jumped on a freight train heading east through the rockies toward Pueblo. On Tuesday morning, the train pulled into Pueblo. Joe, being a loner, walked away from the other three boys. Tuesday night, however, they again found Joe wandering aimlessly in the freight yards, and all four boarded a freight heading back to Grand Junction.

What Joe did that day in Pueblo is not clear. He told the boys that he met his brother and they went to a picture show. He had one brother, George, but later investigations showed that he hadn't seen him for more than six years. Since the Arridy family had moved again, there was no chance that he was with any of his family from Tuesday morning until he left that evening.

Since a Pueblo-to-Grand Junction run usually took twenty-four hours, the foursome arrived back in Grand Junction on Wednesday night, August 12, 1936. As soon as they got off the train, Joe wandered away from the others. He had completed his first successful round-trip train ride. He may have understood that when you get on a freight train going into the mountains, it ended up in Pueblo, his home town. And the Pueblo freight yards were just east of the Bessemer district.

One resident of the home said he saw Joe in Grand Junction on Thursday, August 13. After that, no one heard from Joe until he turned up in the Cheyenne, Wyoming, railroad yards, sixteen days later.

13

SHATTERED FAMILY

It was ten o'clock on August 15, 1936, a warm evening in Pueblo's Bessemer district, and everything was going right for the family of Riley and Peggy Drain. Riley's first wife had died in 1929, and Peggy stepped in as his second—a valued emotional partner as well as a caring and kind stepmother to Dorothy, 15, Barbara, 12, and Billy, 9. Riley signed on with the Works Progress Administration shortly after President Roosevelt cranked it up in 1935 as part of his depression-fighting New Deal. The WPA put hundreds of men to work on public projects such as parks and highways. One year later, Riley was a project supervisor, and his family lived in a comfortable bungalow at 1536 Stone Avenue, across the street from the Bessemer ditch, three blocks southwest of Bessemer Park.

Everyone was happy that night. Riley and Peggy were leaving for a benefit dance at the Anzick night club. They would leave the club at 2 A.M. with another couple, stop for sandwiches and coffee at the Grand Cafe, and head for home at 3 A.M. The three children had big plans, too. Billy left to sleep over with a friend up the street. Dorothy and Barbara had just baked a cake for the next day's Sunday school picnic and placed it in the pantry to cool. On Sunday morning, the girls would walk to Sunday school at the Church of God on Cedar Street, two blocks north of Bessemer Park, and later go to the picnic in the park. The girls hugged and kissed their parents good-bye, then went to their bedroom toward the back of the house. Before Peggy left the house, she hooked the screen to the back door and left a lamp burning in the front room. Riley and Peggy left the front door unlocked.

When the couple returned, the light in the front room was off. Once inside the home, Riley heard a groan. He hurried to the girl's bedroom and turned on the light. On a blood-soaked bed, he found Dorothy, a great gash in the back of her head, one of her eyes blackened and her mouth bruised. She was lying face down on the outside of the bed. Barbara, still groaning, was on the other side of the bed, toward the wall, curled up. She had been struck on the head in the same manner as her sister. Both girls were clad in their nightgowns.

Peggy ran to the girls' grandparents' house next door and called the police.

Coroner C. N. Caldwell would report later that the girls had been struck with a sharp object, possibly a hatchet. Dorothy received a wound behind her ear that was nearly three inches long and had cut into her brain. The black eye and facial bruises showed that the perpetrator also had beaten her severely with his fists. And she had been raped.

The doctors at Saint Mary Corwin Hospital would report that Barbara received two blows, possibly from the blunt edge of the hatchet. Her skull had not been penetrated. She showed no signs of sexual assault, but her condition was "grave." She was in a deep coma not expected to live.

When the police arrived, Riley staggered out of the bungalow with Dorothy in his arms. One glance told the experienced officers that she was beyond aid, and they persuaded the father to carry her back into the house.

14

THE FRENZY

Shortly after the first officers arrived on the crime scene, Police Chief J. Arthur Grady received a call at his home.

It took me a little more than thirty minutes to reach the Drain place. The policemen in charge there had done the best they could but relatives and friends of the family were milling around the house, and everything was excitement and disorder. . . . By 9 A.M. word of the tragedy had spread across the city, and hundreds of excited townspeople were standing in front of the residence. Pueblo has a population of about 50,000 and by 10 A.M. it seemed as though 49,000 of them had swooped down Stone Avenue. I finally ordered the street cleared, and we roped off the block and posted officers to keep traffic moving (Grady, 1936, p. 5).

According to Grady's report of the crime, only the bed was bloody and in disarray. Nothing else in the house had been disturbed. Peggy Drain repeated to officials that she first became alarmed when she saw that the lamp in the living room had been turned off. Next door, Frank Gorshe said he returned from his job at the steel mill at 11:20 P.M. and saw that the kitchen light in the Drain home was burning. It was still on when he went to bed after midnight (TPC, 8-17).

According to officials, the actual time of the murder was vague—maybe late August 15 or early August 16. Obviously, the murderer entered by the front door, turned out the light in the front room, turned on the light in the kitchen, and entered the back bedroom. Since the door to the back bedroom opened close to the kitchen, the perpetrator might have had ample light to carry out his purpose. Then he may have unhooked the screen on the back door and escaped. At some time during or after the crime, the kitchen light was turned off.

The evidence found on Sunday was a heel print on a bed sheet, some smudged fingerprints, and a complete palm print on the bedroom floor. Several footprints also were found around the rear gate which led into the alley (TPC, 8-17). Grady put in a call for bloodhounds, but by the time they arrived on the scene, the crowds made it impossible to follow a scent.

Firemen and highway department workers raked every vacant lot in the area for the murder weapon. Even the Bessemer ditch across the street was drained so that the bottom and sides could be searched.

Grady also reported that earlier on Sunday morning, two separate women reported that a man had tried to attack them unsuccessfully, at different times on Saturday evening:

Probably the same fiend was responsible. [The women] gave the same description of their attempted assailant, and this seemed to bear out our belief. He wore a light shirt, dark trousers and a cap, and he weighed about 135 pounds and was about 5 feet 5 inches tall. In both cases he had seized his intended victims from the rear, and had pinioned their arms, but their screams had frightened him away. One attack was at 11 P.M. Saturday and the other 45 minutes later (pp. 5-6).

On Monday, a $1,000 reward was posted for apprehension of the murderer. Half of the money was put up by the city and the other half by the county.

Two weeks earlier—on Sunday, August 2, at 1443 Cedar Street, just three blocks away—two women in the same bed had been attacked in almost the same manner. As in the Drain case, the perpetrator entered the bedroom while they were sleeping. He killed Sally Crumply, 72, and severely injured Mrs. R. O. McMurtree, 58. The heads of both women had been bludgeoned. The attacks at the Drain and the McMurtree homes took place at approximately the same time in the evening.

MANIAC MURDERS GIRL, 15, BLUDGEONS YOUNGER SISTER screamed headlines on the front page of the Monday, August 17 edition of *The Pueblo Chieftain*. BLOOD-HOUNDS HUNT TRAIL OF CLUB-KILLER; ATTACK IS SECOND IN FORTNIGHT, served as the subtitle. Then came the third sub-head: DOROTHY DRAIN FOUND DEAD BY PARENTS; SISTER, BARBARA, IN CRITICAL CONDITION; FIVE MEN HELD FOR QUESTIONING.

Like all stories that announce a society-ripping tragedy, the story contained a smattering of facts, conjectures, and statements by people on and around the scene—many that proved later to be of no use in the solving of a crime. Five Pueblo suspects were named, along with a printed description of their suspicious activities.

Also on the front page, came a nudging editorial:

THESE BRUTAL CRIMES MUST BE SOLVED
AN EDITORIAL
Pueblo's most vicious and brutal crimes of modern times go into the records, a challenge to city and county law enforcement bodies. Written in the blood of two aged women and Dorothy and Barbara Drain, these crimes leave one sick at the thought that they can happen in our community.

Enforcement officers charged with the duty of running down the fiend abroad in our midst are now bending every effort in a ceaseless drive to bring him to cover. They must know that an outraged citizenry will not yield to anything but a sustained, exhaustive search for this arch criminal until he is found and fittingly punished.

At this writing they faced a monumental task. They are entitled to fair play from the public, a reasonable exercise of time and effort to sift clues and match evidence. Public harassment does not serve the need of the times but cooperative procedure will make for results.

It strikes us that should the local officials reach the blank wall that is so often encountered here as elsewhere in such cases, they should call upon the best criminal minds in other cities for assistance.

In a word, here is a case on which all of us must stand agreed—A CASE THAT CANNOT BE ALLOWED TO REST.

The Associated Press filed similar stories that appeared in almost every newspaper in Colorado and surrounding states. All police departments in the region—towns like Walsenburg, Denver, Sterling, Limon, and Greeley—took into custody every known "peeping tom," vagrant, mental patient, and sex criminal they could find on their streets.

In Englewood, Joseph Qualiteri, an escaped mental patient from the Pueblo State Hospital, resisted arrest and was shot to death by an officer. Later, it was confirmed that Qualiteri was not involved in the Pueblo murders.

For the next ten days, *The Pueblo Chieftain* reported everything it learned about the case—which wasn't really very much. What it could report usually appeared in the headlines:

AUGUST 18:

POLICE SIFT MANY CLUES IN BLUDGEONING
BRUTAL MURDER STILL A MYSTERY
Two More Men Held for Questioning in Case
Two Other Potential Suspects Provide Iron Clad Alibis

AUGUST 19:

NEW LEADS SPUR PROBE OF DRAIN MURDER
FIVE OUT OF SIX SUSPECTS HELD FOR QUESTIONING BY POLICE GAIN LIBERTY
      WITH ALIBIS
Condition of Dead Girl's Sister Reported As Highly Precarious
Date for Inquest Still Undecided

AUGUST 20:

TWO NEW SUSPECTS HUNTED IN BRUTAL SLAYING OF CHILD
Officials Decline to Reveal Identity of Men Sought
Hundreds of Mourners View Dead Girl's Body

AUGUST 21-23: No Stories

AUGUST 24:

MURDER CASE UNSOLVED, THO OFFICERS REPORT PROGRESS
No Major Developments Reported Over Week End
Officials Deny Mystery Has Been Given Up as Defying Solution

On Tuesday, August 25, and Wednesday, August 26, no stories about the case appeared in *The Chieftain*. The officers were running out of suspects. The case was growing cold. But it would not stay that way.

15

CHEYENNE SURPRISE

Nine days after the crime, on Wednesday evening, August 26, Pueblo Police Chief Grady received an unsettling call from an old friend.

I was summoned to the telephone to talk with Sheriff George J. Carroll of Cheyenne, Wyoming, and when I heard his words I all but dropped the telephone receiver.

"Chief Grady," he said, "we are holding a fellow here who says he killed the little Drain girl in your city. He's a nut—he can't even read or write—and he's told us two or three different stories. But he seems to know all about the Drain murder, and I wouldn't be surprised if he is the man you want" (Grady, 1936, p. 34).

Joe Arridy had been arrested for loitering in the Union Pacific railroad yards. Railroad detectives George Burnett and Carl Christianson spied the vagrant and arrested him. *The Pueblo Chieftain* set the arrest time at 5:00 P.M.; the *Wyoming State Tribune* reported 5:30. Since Joe was wearing a khaki shirt, the detectives thought he was an army deserter from Fort Logan, Colorado. But once they talked to him, they concluded that he was "a feebleminded moron." By the time the detectives delivered Joe to Sheriff Carroll, they saw him as some kind of joke. "Here's a fellow you ought to talk to, all right," they said laughingly to Sheriff Carroll (Grady, p. 35).

But Sheriff Carroll did interrogate Joe. An hour and a half later, he telephoned Pueblo. Then he talked to the press. The first stories of Joe Arridy's confession appeared in the next day's newspapers. Since Sheriff Carroll did not take notes, and the confessions were never written down or signed by Joe, all the alleged admissions were broadcast to the world, and they kept changing. The most thorough story appeared in *The Pueblo Chieftain* (Thursday, August 27). The key statements:

Sheriff George Carroll of Cheyenne said that Arddy voluntarily confessed that he attacked the girls. Asked why he killed the older girl, Arddy was quoted as replying, "Just for meanness."

He said, according to Carroll, that after bludgeoning the two girls he assaulted the older one twice.

Arddy, according to Sheriff Carroll, said he entered the Drain home about 11 o'clock the night of August 15 after he had seen the girls' parents, Mr. and Mrs. Riley A. Drain, leave the house.

On entering, he struck a match and found his way to a light switch and went directly to the room where the two girls were sleeping. He said he struck them with a hatchet.

Arddy, the sheriff said, was unable to say where he got the hatchet.

Sheriff Carroll said he gave three Pueblo addresses as his own, but no such addresses exist. Arddy said he lived at 1791 Routt, and later changed his statement saying he lived at 1640 and 7733 Routt.

He accurately described the girls' positions in the bed and their night clothing and many details about the Drain home, but at no time did he ever give his correct address.

At first he told Sheriff Carroll that he had beaten the girls with a club. He then changed his story and said that he used a hatchet and after going to his own home, buried the hatchet between the house and the barn. At another time he said he hid the hatchet in a haystack.

After attacking the Drain girls and leaving the Drain home he went to his own home. There, he said, he was severely beaten by his mother and sister, who then imprisoned him in an upstairs room where they kept him for eight days.

Escaping from the house, he said, he caught a freight train out of the city, stopped in Denver to see a brother who is a railroader and to seek work, and arrived in Cheyenne last night.

All of Arddy's statements were made before Sheriff Carroll and Elmer D. Brown, under sheriff.

Accompanying this first story was a posed photograph of Sheriff Carroll and Grady, taken in 1935 at Atlantic City during the "Police Chiefs" Convention. Carroll is seated and Grady is standing, his elbow resting on his friend's shoulders.

Almost all of Joe's statements in the early confession were proved false within the next few days. Carroll also claimed that at no time did he find Joe a "suggestible" person, one who would try to please an authority figure by giving the answers he thought the sheriff wanted to hear. Under Sheriff Elmer D. Brown's corroboration would have helped, but his name never came up in this case again. Carroll testified later that he was alone when he interrogated Joe until three officials from Pueblo arrived.

Carroll's statements about what he heard Arridy say was punctuated by a short summarizing article in *The Chieftain* as well:

MAN IS UNDOUBTEDLY INSANE, SAYS SHERIFF

Sheriff George Carroll of Cheyenne, Wyo., told *The Chieftain* Wednesday night by long distance telephone that Joe Arrdy, held there after admitting the slaying of Dorothy Drain, is undoubtedly insane.

The sheriff said that Arrdy told a lurid story of after having killed the Drain girl and critically bludgeoning her sister, he assaulted the older girl twice.

"I am very sorry for what I did," the sheriff quoted Arrdy as saying.

Carroll said Arrdy was picked up as a straggler in the Cheyenne railroad yards about 5 P.M. and that when questioned at headquarters he told officers he was from Pueblo. The officers then began questioning him as a possible suspect in the Drain murder, and he launched into a fairly coherent account of how he entered the Drain home and attacked the two girls.

He said Arrdy told him he entered the house thru an open door and found the two girls in their bed. At first he said he attacked the girls with a club and later told the sheriff that he used a hatchet. Afterward he attacked the older girl twice.

Sheriff Carroll said that many of the details told by Arrdy checked with actual happenings in the Drain home, but that Arrdy was unable to give his own address.

"To all appearances he is unquestionably insane," the sheriff said. He was described as 21 years of age, dark complected and Italian. He was wearing a khaki shirt, big blue overalls, old shoes and was carrying a skull cap in his pocket.

Immediately after Carroll's call, Detectives Everett Horne and W. L. McDonald, along with District Attorney French L. Taylor, drove to Cheyenne. Chief Grady rushed officers to the Arridy home at 1604 Cedar Street, in hope of finding a weapon and other incriminating evidence. Since the house was in the middle of the Bessemer district's bungalows, they found no upstairs room, no barn, and no haystack. There was an attic, but it was closed off and undisturbed. Henry and Mary Arridy, George, 14, and Amelia, 12, swore that they had not seen Joe since he went away six years ago. Neighbors and others who knew the Arridys said they hadn't seen Joe either. The officers also learned that Joe did not have a railroader brother in Denver.

Although it wasn't mentioned in the paper, the Arridys lived at 1708 Pine when their son was taken to Grand Junction. Since then they had lived in other homes before moving to Cedar Street. So even if Joe had tried, he probably couldn't have found them.

But other Pueblo citizens—plenty of them—found the Arridy home. According to *The Chieftain:*

Thousands of the residents of the city, keyed to a high pitch since the brutal murder, gathered around the Arddy home as police began their investigation there about 8 P.M. Firemen roped off the block to keep the throngs back. As in the day following the murder, excitement ran high and mob spirit was feared.

Chief Grady ordered the Arridy family taken into custody.

Grady also gave a second-hand quote to the press that heightened a repulsive characterization of Joe Arridy: "Dr. Jefferson, superintendent of the mental home for defectives from which Arrdy escaped, told Chief Grady that young Arddy is a 'bad actor' and a sexual pervert." Grady used this statement as his finishing touch in his first meeting with the press. That statement would haunt Superintendent Jefferson after he gathered his wits and become an advocate for his former resident.

"THERE'LL BE NO LYNCHING," GRADY RULES, was the banner headline on the next day's paper (TPC, 8-28).

Although Chief Grady was highly vocal to the press, an earth-shaking secret was being withheld from them. It was this secret that made the chief almost drop the telephone when Sheriff Carroll first called. The secret, of course, was shared with Carroll, and of course it influenced the remainder of his interrogations of Joe.

16

Famous Sheriff

Fifty-six-year-old Sheriff George Carroll was a 28-year veteran in the Laramie County sheriff's office. He started as a deputy in 1908 and was elected to the top post in 1921. According to a historical piece in the May 19, 1961, *Cheyenne Eagle*, Carroll was highly respected in law-enforcement circles throughout the Rocky Mountain region.

Carroll helped with the breakup of the notorious Barker gang. In 1928, after one of his deputies was murdered by the gang on a county road just outside Cheyenne, Carroll packed his bag and joined a posse with other police officers and federal agents. For 40 days they chased the gang from state to state, until they succeeded in "eliminating 22 members of the gang—including Ma Barker—either by bullets or jail sentences."

In 1933 he joined another task force in search of the kidnapped Claude K. Boettcher II, scion of a wealthy Denver family. It was Carroll and a Wyoming Highway Patrol officer who found the kidnap gang's hideout and secured Boettcher's release.

So when Carroll announced a possible break in the Drain case, Chief Grady listened. Then, after Carroll's statements reached the outraged citizens of Pueblo, he became their hero. This sudden interest in the Cheyenne sheriff moved *The Chieftain* to find out how Carroll got the confession from Joe Arridy:

> An incident that provided only a joke for other officers gave Sheriff George Carroll of Cheyenne, Wyo., the "lead" which culminated in Joe Arridy's confession of the brutal murder and assault upon Dorothy Drain.
>
> This revelation was made by the Wyoming sheriff early yesterday in an interview with *The Chieftain* as he outlined step by step the manner in which the 21-year-old sex-pervert confessed the act which has aroused Pueblo as no other crime has done.
>
> Between the lines of Carroll's account was eloquent testimony to his shrewdness in drawing a fairly coherent statement of the murder from the feeble-minded youth whose warped brain responded clearly on only one subject—women. . . .
>
> When Arridy was picked up late Wednesday afternoon for loitering in the Cheyenne railroad yards, he was at first held in custody in the yard office where a group of special officers and others quickly saw that he was a feeble-minded moron—the type that is often the butt of jokes and gibes.
>
> When Sheriff Carroll walked into the office they laughingly told him, "Here is a fellow you ought to talk to."
>
> But it was no joking matter for Sheriff Carroll. He is a stickler for detail. He questioned even

the lowliest vagrant and the information is stored away in his retentive mind for future reference if it is needed.

"Where are you from, son?" he asked the loiterer from the railroad yards.

Arridy said he was from Pueblo.

Sheriff Carroll had a pretty thorough knowledge of the sex slaying of the Drain girl. The whole thing flashed thru his mind. The feeble-minded youth fitted the picture.

The sheriff asked him a number of routine questions and presently began to talk to him about women, not about any particular women—just women in general.

Then for the first time Arridy began to show interest, to respond with some animation in the questioning. He talked freely about women, egged on by the sheriff's casual questions and remarks.

Suddenly the sheriff asked him:

"If you like women so well, why do you hurt them?"

"I didn't intend to," was Arridy's reply.

Those were the words that clinched Joe Arridy as the No. 1 suspect in the Drain murder.

Sheriff Carroll halted his questioning and took Arridy to his own office.

He kept him on the one subject to which his animal impulses reacted. He asked him if he had any sweethearts in Pueblo, what women he knew there, what their names were.

Casually he approached the matter of the Drain murder, touched some responsive spot in the twisted, degenerate brain. Readily this low mentality responded and the craven youth told the sheriff he had killed the Drain girls.

The admission came in a matter-of-fact voice as if the youth attached no more importance to it than he had to the statement that he had come from Pueblo.

With equal unconcern he added detail after detail, and as the questioning continued more intensively, began to make contradictory statements, to bog down sometimes in a complicated skein of events which obviously had left some confusion in his defective mind. But always the main thread of his story held true to the major details of the crime.

What subsequently happened is now history.

But the record will show that the turning point in the investigation of Pueblo's most loathsome crime came when a shrewd officer discovered the perverted and sensual path followed by the workings of the feeble and moronic mind of a man who appeared to be nothing more than a vagrant (Guest, 1936a).

There was no doubt in Carroll's mind that Joe Arridy was the murderer of Dorothy Drain.

17

THE SECRET

The deep secret that Pueblo Police Chief Grady harbored at the time of the Cheyenne sheriff's first call was this: Grady believed that he already had the murderer of Dorothy Drain in custody. His name was Frank Aguilar, a five-foot-five Mexican national who lived with his family at 211 Division, nine blocks east of the crime scene. Officers quietly arrested him on Wednesday, August 20, during Dorothy Drain's funeral. Grady found the murder weapon at Aguilar's house. All he needed now was Aguilar's confession. But Aguilar refused to confess. He vehemently denied having anything to do with the crime.

Then it all came out in *The Chieftain* on September 3, after Joe, in a later interrogation, was questioned about an accomplice and allegedly said that a man named Frank was with him. Consequently, Joe provided the confession they could not extract from Aguilar. With that, the secret of Frank Aguilar came out of the bag.

Overlooking no possibility of tracking down the Drain murderers, Chief of Police J. Arthur Grady and others working on the case assigned officers to be on the lookout at the funeral of 15-year-old Dorothy Drain, five days after she was slain in her bedroom.

Assigned to the funeral watch were Officers Nick J. Mikatich and R. Earl Butler. And some quirk of a distorted mind drew the killer to the funeral of his victim.

Mikatich saw Aguilar loitering about in the crowd of mourners outside the funeral chapel. He was dressed in overalls and rough clothes and looked out of place in such a scene.

Mikatich had a hunch. "There's the killer," he said to Butler.

A moment later Aguilar walked over to the two officers and told them that he wanted to find Riley Drain—the father of the murdered girl.

With suspicions already aroused, Butler and Mikatich began to question the man and he told them he was a friend of the Drain family. To other leading questions he replied that he had worked under Drain on a WPA project, that he had been in the Drain home, that he knew the two Drain girls by their first names.

Butler and Mikatich then called Assistant District Attorney Joe Botelman and Deputy Richard Cooper—who also were on the "funeral watch"—and conferred with them. Together they took Aguilar into custody and hustled him off to jail.

In the meantime Chief Grady and his detectives had put Aguilar at the top of the suspect list and had a mass of circumstantial evidence against him. His strange action at the funeral confirmed previous suspicions.

The police disclosed yesterday that as their systematic investigation got underway they had carefully checked a list of some 100 men who had worked under Riley Drain, a WPA supervisor. Among the group were several who had been discharged from Drain's project, and one of these was Aguilar.

All were checked for the possibilities of a revenge motive in the attack upon Drain's daughters.

On the third day after the murder, it was disclosed last night, an incident occurred which definitely placed Aguilar among the most suspicious.

Aguilar approached Riley Drain and handed him some five-cent coins, telling him they were from his (Aguilar's) mother, who thought they "might be of some help to the family." Drain reported the incident to the police.

After his arrest Aguilar stoutly denied any knowledge of the crime during several periods of relentless questioning. But police had sufficient circumstantial evidence to strongly link him with the case. He was held, and one by one other suspects were released. Officers, detectives, and the district attorney's staff believed they were on the right track and all were closely cooperating.

Then came the discovery of the hatchet at Aguilar's home which his confession now proves was used in the crime.

The hatchet, although washed of blood, had peculiar nicks in it which added another link to the chain of evidence. Photographs were made of the wounds on the Drain girls' heads and were enlarged to actual size. The photographs plainly showed the marks left by the nicks in the hatchet, matched it perfectly.

Thus it was that the Pueblo police had quietly developed a nearly iron-bound case against [Aguilar] (Guest, 1936b).

It was *nearly* iron-clad because there was no confession. So Joe, in a sense, did for Aguilar what he refused to do himself.

18

THE MESHING

Suddenly all the facts involving Joe Arridy and Frank Aguilar needed to be pulled together quickly. Now the Pueblo police provided a steady stream of facts to *The Pueblo Chieftain*.

FRIDAY, AUGUST 28 EDITION

Arridy Buys a Gun?

Several facts established by police Thursday tended to substantiate Arridy's story. One was the discovery that a pistol was purchased here the day before the Drain murder by a man giving the name of "Joseph Arridy," identified thru a newspaper photograph last night as the Joe Arridy who has confessed to the crime.

The gun was purchased at the David S. Kahn pawnshop at 219 South Union Avenue and was sold to the man by Saul Kahn, son of the proprietor.

This identification was regarded by officers as highly important, inasmuch as it definitely shows that Arridy was in Pueblo at the time of the slaying.

After the purchase of the gun had been reported to police Thursday morning by young Kahn, following his reading of a newspaper account of Arridy's arrest at Cheyenne, officers there were asked to question Arridy about this matter. "He readily admitted buying the gun," Chief Grady said.

This statement became bothersome right off. Could things have moved so fast? The interrogations did not conclude in Cheyenne until around Thursday noon. The story did not come out in *The Chieftain* until the afternoon of that day. So what paper could Mr. Kahn have read? And what news photograph could he have seen? The Thursday edition printed only a large photograph of Sheriff Carroll and Chief Grady. A first photo of Joe was finally published in the edition that included Kahn's visit to the police station.

Where did he get the money for the gun? Residents of the home in Grand Junction were not allowed to have money. Judging from the way Joe functioned in the world and the way he reacted to it, how does purchasing a gun even begin to fit with his passive nature? And then what happened to the gun? And since Joe's formal first name was Joe, and he called himself Joe, why would Kahn have said that he gave the name *Joseph?*

As for Joe's confessions, he was confessing to everything they asked. He confessed to the complete crime in the Drain home. Later, he revised that confession to include Aguilar. He confessed to attacking Irene O'Driscoll in Colorado Springs. He told Carroll he tried to attack at least one woman in Pueblo around 11 o'clock, on the night of the Drain murder. If that was true, where was Aguilar? And how could Joe still arrive at the Drain home at 11 o'clock? How did he even know it *was* 11 o'clock?

So Joe confessed and confessed and confessed. That's just the way Joe was.

Arridy Buys Pants in Pueblo?

"The youth told officers at Cheyenne that he bought a pair of blue corduroy trousers at the Montgomery Ward & Company store here on Aug. 14 for $2.95." A spokesman at the store said that a pair of blue corduroys was sold at that exact price, but the store records, of course, did not show to whom the sale was made. Again it was not clear where Joe got his money. It was also unclear how Joe—who in his earlier intelligence test failed to count 13 pennies and could not repeat four digits after they were spoken to him—now could recall the exact price of $2.95. And, like the gun, what happened to the pants?

District Attorney Gives Hints About an Accomplice

District Attorney Taylor said he was investigating "an indication" from Arridy that he was not alone when he committed the crime. According to Taylor, that investigation began Thursday evening:

"From our talk with this man," Taylor said, "we deem it advisable to check further. From his story it seems another man is implicated and we have requested his arrest. I feel sure this man can be located."

"This boy," Taylor said, "has told us his story over and over again. I believe he is telling the truth. But we must check out every detail for we are dealing with a maniac, and we cannot accept his statements upon their face."

Aguilar, of course, was already in custody when Taylor made this statement.

SATURDAY, AUGUST 29 EDITION

Arridy Rushed to Pueblo Thursday Night

"Cloaked in the deepest secrecy," Sheriff Carroll and Cheyenne Chief of Police T. Joe Cahill, as well as Pueblo officials Taylor, Horne, and McDonald brought Joe to Pueblo. He was quietly housed at the Colorado State Hospital. It didn't happen that way, but that's what the paper said.

Crime "Reenacted" on Friday

Held at the State hospital until about 1:30 P.M., Arridy was taken from the institution by a squad of officers, including Sheriff Carroll, Chief Cahill, Taylor, Grady, Undersheriff Earl H. Dunlap of Pueblo, and Detectives Horne, McDonald, and Richard Anderson.

Arridy was taken to the scene of the crime in the rear seat of an officer's car. Another carload of officers in another machine followed close behind.

To make sure there would be no slip-up, several officers patrolled the neighborhood of the Drain home both before and while the reenactment of the crime was in progress. . . .

Arridy, Taylor said, traced in detail his movements on the night of the crime. First, he showed the officers where he and Aguilar, whom he knows only as "Frank," waited in the darkness on the Bessemer ditch bridge at Stone and Bay State avenues until the girls' father and their step-mother, Mrs. Peggy Drain left the home.

Arridy said he and his companion walked down to the alley, up to the Drain backyard, entering it thru a back-fence gate. After watching the girls thru the window for a time, Arridy declared they entered the house through the front door.

Then the youth traced his movements inside the house, pointing out where he had turned on the lights and how they made their way to the girls' bedroom. On one point Arridy told conflicting stories. He claimed Friday afternoon that Aguilar struck both girls with a handleless hatchet as they lay asleep, although previously he had confessed to striking the blows himself.

Friday, officers quoted him as saying Aguilar struck both of them, rendering them unconscious. Then he is said to have admitted that first Aguilar and then he criminally assaulted the older girl. They left by the front door of the house, he claimed.

Kahn Identifies Joe as Gun Purchaser

Hurried away from the Drain home, Arridy was taken to police headquarters. There he was brought face-to-face with pawnbroker Saul Kahn, who "positively identified him as the youth to whom he sold a cheap automatic pistol on the day preceding the murder."

Arridy Identifies Aguilar

Then Aguilar was brought into the room.
"Do you know this man?" asked District Attorney Taylor.
"That's Frank," Arridy replied. . . .
Evidence previously obtained by officers pointed to Aguilar as Arridy's companion and the identification Friday was regarded merely as the final link in a chain of circumstances connecting Aguilar with the crime.

Arridy Quiet But Aguilar Speaks Out

According to the police, in spite of the confrontation, Aguilar vehemently denied ever meeting Joe Arridy. He also denied having anything to do with the Drain murder. "In contrast to the silent, moody Arridy, Aguilar has been willing to talk at all times, police said, but has steadfastly maintained his innocence. He has claimed to officers that he went to bed at 8:30 P.M. on the night of Aug. 15."

Aguilar and Arridy Rushed to Canon City

After the confrontation, the two men were rushed to the Colorado State Penitentiary for safekeeping. The machine in which the two men were taken to Canon City was one of the crack automobiles of the courtesy patrol's fleet. It was driven by Pueblo district supervisor of the state highway patrol, William R. Welsh, Jr. Two other officers accompanied him, while another carload of officials followed. Still included in the entourage were the sheriff and chief of police from Cheyenne.

Police Find Hairs

One statement in the day's news came as a surprise:

Another piece of evidence heretofore kept secret by authorities are several hairs which were found on the sheets of the bed in which the girls were attacked. These, along with samples of hair from both Arridy and Aguilar, have been sent to a laboratory at Denver for a comparison, Taylor said last night.

SUNDAY, AUGUST 30 EDITION

Arridy Accused of Assault in Springs

So announced the front-page headline.

Chief Hugh D. Harper of the Colorado Springs police department said that the girl who beat off her assailant on August 23 as she was walking home from work . . . is willing to go to Canon City Sunday and view Arridy. . . .

The girl, Irene O'Driscoll, 20, a telephone company employee, said she scratched the hands of her assailant in seeking to escape from him.

The identification was made by Miss O'Driscoll from a newspaper picture of Arridy, Chief Harper said, after the description of the man who attacked her fitted that of Arridy in every detail, even to the overalls he wore when arrested in Cheyenne Wednesday.

Chief Harper will accompany Miss O'Driscoll to the Canon City Penitentiary Sunday in an effort to make a positive identification.

Arridy Family Released

On Saturday evening, District Attorney Taylor ordered the release of Henry and Mary Arridy, as well as their son George, and daughter, Amelia. For three days the family had been questioned, until the police were convinced that Joe had not been home for the past six years.

Barbara Drain Regains Consciousness

The 13-year-old returned to complete consciousness and talked freely with her father. The attending physician said she appeared completely rational and her chances for recovery are excellent.

MONDAY, AUGUST 31 EDITION

Cheyenne Sheriff Produces Bloody Shirt

On Sunday evening, after returning from Canon City, Sheriff Carroll phoned Chief Grady and told him about the recovery of a white shirt. According to Carroll, Arridy had discarded it at the camp of a railroad "extra gang." There was a large rip in the back and a quantity of blood *on the inside of the shirt*. Also stamped on the inside of the shirt in indelible ink was the name, "Peter Clauson."

Grady then telephoned Superintendent Jefferson and learned that Peter Clauson is another "patient at the institution," and Arridy apparently obtained his fellow patient's shirt at some time before running away from the institution.

Although it was not mentioned to the press earlier, Grady now said that Joe had confessed that "he completely undressed before he criminally assaulted the Drain girl. The youth got the blood on the inside of the shirt when he put it back on, Grady believes."

How the shirt was torn and when he exchanged it for the khaki shirt still remained a mystery.

Arridy in Cheyenne from August 20 to 26

In his Sunday evening call, Carroll told Grady that "it has been definitely established that Arridy arrived in Cheyenne a week before his arrest. This fact also was established at the camp of the railroad extra gang, where workers told the sheriff that a man they are certain was Arridy arrived at their camp Aug. 20 and stayed until Aug. 26."

Colorado Springs Case Against Arridy Fizzles

Chief Hugh Harper and Irene O'Driscoll arrived Sunday at the penitentiary in Canon City, along with Colorado Springs Deputy District Attorney Thomas I. Purcell. When she viewed his picture earlier, she was sure that Arridy was her assailant, "in every detail, even to the overalls he wore." Now, however, the police reported that O'Driscoll said that "he looked like the man and walked like him," but failed to make a positive identification.

What Chief Harper failed to tell the press was that Joe couldn't have attacked Miss O'Driscoll, because it was now clear that he was in Cheyenne at the time of the attack on August 23.

Another Grand Junction Resident in Cheyenne?

In another phase of the officers' effort to definitely check every possible part of Arridy's oral confession, the patient who escaped with him from the Grand Junction institution will be questioned in detail this week, Police Chief Grady said.

The patient who escaped with Arridy is Clifford Mullins who was recaptured last Friday at Hot Sulphur Springs. After his capture, Mullins said he and Arridy separated shortly after their escape, and that he had made his way to his home in Hot Sulphur Springs after going to Salt Lake City, Cheyenne, and Denver.

Because Mullins admitted being in Cheyenne, officers wish to determine if he and Arridy were there at the same time.

WEDNESDAY, SEPTEMBER 2 EDITION

Institution's Board President Doubts Arridy Committed Crime

After taking part in another investigation, Val Higgins, President of the Board of Control of the State Homes for Mental Defectives in both Grand Junction and Ridge expressed doubt that Joe could have committed the crime.

Police Say Arridy in Pueblo on Day Before Crime

The police based their contention on two factors. The press was reminded that pawn-broker Saul Kahn had identified Joe as being in the shop on the day before the murder. Second, "officers maintain that no one save the actual slayer could know details of the crime that have been revealed by Arridy."

❑ ❑ ❑

And so it went. Little did the readers of *The Chieftain* know that while they were reading the last two articles, Frank Aguilar had signed a confession stating that he killed Dorothy Drain.

19

THE "X"

In 1966, the Supreme Court ruled, in *Miranda v. Arizona*, that "nothing arrested persons say can be used against them in their trial unless they have been told they have certain rights." For example, suspects must be told they have the right to remain silent, that anything they say can be held against them. They also must be told that they can have a lawyer present during questioning and, if they cannot afford one, the court will appoint one. If a suspect requests an attorney, the questioning must cease until an attorney is present.

More police departments are tape-recording the interrogations of persons suspected of committing heinous crimes. This trend should continue until continuous sound and video cameras are used. Otherwise, there is no real record of what really goes on between police officers and a suspect.

But this was Wednesday, September 2, 1936, in the Colorado State Penitentiary at Canon City, and there was *no record* of what went on during the interrogation. Frank Aguilar was there "for safekeeping"—to ward off a lynching in Pueblo. Guilty or innocent, Aguilar was legally naked. He went into what was conceivably his fifth day of questioning. It was him against all the officials who day after day cajoled and confronted him. Since no outside observers were present, it was Aguilar's words against the words of his accusers.

On that Wednesday morning, District Attorney French Taylor said that Aguilar maintained his customary stubborn, silent attitude during the opening hours of the grilling. He denied any connection with the crime. Again and again, he denied ever knowing Joe Arridy.

As the questioning began in the afternoon, according to Taylor, "Arridy was brought in and again told his story, implicating Aguilar, in Aguilar's presence. He looked directly at Aguilar as he told of the plan, the attack, and the escape from the Drain home." Interestingly, Arridy, the man who was usually characterized as an imbecile who spoke in short, incomplete sentences, was portrayed by interrogators as highly verbal and well-focused when they needed detailed incriminating statements from him. They consigned him to the shadows when they didn't need such statements.

After Arridy's so-called confrontation, the questioners focused tightly on Aguilar. They reminded him of the axe found in his home, showed him that it matched the wounds in Dorothy's head. At about this time, according to Taylor, Aguilar blurted out, "If I say 'yes' you'll hang me" (TPC, 10-3).

Shortly afterward, according to Taylor, Aguilar broke and told *everything.* Five legal-sized typewritten pages were produced from what he was supposed to have said.

"Aguilar's confession, signed after hours of questioning by District Attorney French L. Taylor, Warden Roy Best of the penitentiary, and Detectives W. L. McDonald and Everette Horne, corresponds in every detail with the statement of Joe Arridy, young mental defective, made first to Sheriff George Carroll in Cheyenne, Wyo., a week ago" (Osborne, 1936).

During the actual confession-obtaining interrogations of the afternoon, it appears that Joe was either not present or was a very silent onlooker. Not once did the confession contain any statements by him. It was strictly Aguilar and his questioners. Since Aguilar could not read or write, he placed an "X" at the end of the five pages.

The complete confession appeared in *The Chieftain* on September 3:

State of Colorado
Fremont County
Canon City

I, Frank Aguilar, do hereby freely and voluntarily make the following statements:

Q. When you were on the corner that night at the Minnequa bank you saw two men talking?
A. Yes.
Q. You don't know these men do you?
A. No.
Q. One of them was a Mexican, what was the other one?
A. The other man was not an American, kind of Irish or some other people.
Q. And you heard them say?
A. I heard them say that Riley was going to the dance. I wasn't sure they were going out.
Q. When were you sure they were going out?
A. When I see him leave.
Q. After you heard this at the corner you went over home and after going home you came back on Northern, when you got back on Northern you met Joe?
A. Not at that time. It was later.
Q. When you met Joe, then you and Joe talked about going up and attacking these girls, is that right?
A. Yes sir.
Q. After you had talked about going and attacking these girls, you then went home, you and Joe went back to the house?
A. Yes.
Q. While you and Joe were at the house you got the hatchet?
A. Yes.
Q. Then where did you get the hatchet?
A. In my house.
Q. Where did you get it?
A. Right where you found it.
Q. After you got the hatchet you and Joe went over to Mr. Drain's house?
A. The back.
Q. How did you get in the yard?
A. Thru the gate.
Q. You went thru the back gate?

A. Yes.

Q. When you and Joe went in the back gate, where did you go?

A. Inside.

Q. Did you and Joe hide there in the bushes?

A. Yes sir.

Q. Could you see the girls thru the shadows?

A. Yes.

Q. After you got there and hid in the bushes a few minutes, did Mr. and Mrs. Drain leave?

A. I heard the door slam.

Q. Did you see them leave then?

A. No.

Q. Which way did the car go?

A. I don't remember which way the car went. I just remember the lights.

Q. You saw the car leave the house?

A. Yes.

Q. When the car left the house, was there a light on in the girls' bedroom?

A. Not for a little while.

Q. After the folks left, was there a light on in the girls' room at that time?

A. Yes.

Q. How long was it before the light went out in the girls' room?

A. About 20 or 25 minutes.

Q. How long did you wait after the light went out to the girls' room before you went in the house?

A. Long enough to let them go to sleep.

Q. When you tried to get in the house, which door did you try first?

A. The back one.

Q. Could you get in the back door?

A. No.

Q. Why?

A. Because it was locked.

Q. Then where did you go?

A. Around to the front door.

Q. Was the front door locked?

A. No.

Q. Did you go in the front door?

A. Yes.

Q. When you went in the front door was there a light on?

A. No.

Q. Did you turn a light on?

A. No, lit a match.

Q. Did you turn a light off in the room that was entered? You lit a match?

A. Yes.

Q. Then you went thru the house by matches?

A. Yes.

Q. Until you got in the girls' room?

A. Yes.

Q. Was the door open to the girls' room?

A. Yes.

Q. When you went into the girls' room were they asleep?
A. Yes.
Q. When you got in the girls' room, did you turn on a light?
A. Yes.
Q. Did you turn on the light before you hit them in the head?
A. No.
Q. Which girl did you hit on the head first?
A. The big one.
Q. Did you hit the little girl on the head right away?
A. No.
Q. After you hit the big girl on the head did you turn on the light before you assaulted the girls?
A. No.
Q. While you were assaulting the big girl did the little girl awaken?
A. Yes.
Q. When the little girl woke up did she say anything?
A. She said, "Get out."
Q. When the little girl said "Get out" what did you do?
A. I hit her.
Q. How many times.
A. Once first.
Q. Were you assaulting the big girl then?
A. Yes.
Q. And then you reached over with your left hand and hit the little girl?
A. Yes.
Q. Where did you hit the little girl?
A. On the back of the head.
Q. You hit her with the blunt side of the hatchet?
A. Yes.
Q. Then what did you do?
A. When I hit her?
Q. Yes, when you hit her?
A. Finished what I was doing.
Q. You finished what you were doing, you finished assaulting the big girl?
A. Yes.
Q. When you got up from finishing assaulting the big girl what did Joe do?
A. I got out on the side.
Q. Then Joe assaulted the big girl, didn't he?
A. Yes.
Q. Did you assault the big girl again?
A. No.
Q. After Joe got through assaulting the girl what did you do to her?
A. I hit her.
Q. That was when you hit her with the sharp part of the hatchet.
A. Yes.
Q. After you hit the big girl with the sharp part of the hatchet what did you and Joe do?
A. Got out.
Q. How did you get out of the house?
A. Through the front door.

Q. When you went out of the front how did you leave the yard?
A. Between the houses.
Q. Did you go through the Drain's yard?
A. Yes.
Q. How did you get out of the yard?
A. The same way we came in.
Q. Through the gate?
A. Yes.
Q. When you went out of the back gate did you turn to the right up the alley?
A. Yes.
Q. You went up through the end of the alley around the post and out the other alley, didn't you?
A. Yes.
Q. Who was carrying the hatchet?
A. I don't remember.
Q. When you got to the end of the alley which way did you go?
A. When we got into the alley we went right on home.
Q. You cut across the lot and went across to your house?
A. Yes.
Q. When you got home what did you do with the hatchet?
A. Put it in a basket.
Q. After you got home did you wash the hatchet?
A. Yes.
Q. Where?
A. At the pump.
Q. Did you put it at the side of the house in the basket?
A. Yes.
Q. Was Joe with you then?
A. Yes.
Q. Did Joe stay with you all night or did he leave?
A. He left.
Q. Frank, did the hatchet have a handle on it?
A. No.
Q. Did it have anything broken on the hammer part?
A. Yes.
Q. Was that the hatchet I showed you at the police station at Pueblo?
A. Yes.
Q. Did you tell your wife about any of this?
A. No.

Questioned by Warden Roy Best, state penitentiary:

Q. Did you know the girl was dead when you left?
A. No.
Q. When did you first know the girl was dead? Did you buy a newspaper the next morning?
A. No, Sunday morning I went to Hamers.
Q. Did you tell Joe to keep quiet about this?
A. Yes.

Q. You didn't know the girl was dead until you got back from Hamers.
A. Not until Monday morning.

Requestioned by Mr. Taylor:

Q. Did you see Joe after that?
A. No.
Q. Why did you mark the 15th of August on the calendar?
A. Just before I told you before why I marked it.
Q. About tobacco. Are you telling me the truth?
A. Yes, about tobacco.
Q. What kind of pants did you have on when you went over to the Drain's house?
A. I had the same pants I had on at the police station.
Q. It was the pair that was washed?
A. Yes.
Q. The pair that had the blood in the pocket here? (Motioning to right hip pocket)
A. Yes.
Q. That's where you kept the axe in the pocket?
A. Yes.
Q. The shirt had a drop of blood on it, didn't it?
A. Yes a drop of blood.
Q. The shirt that was taken down to the police station and shown to you with one drop of blood on the right sleeve was the one you wore over to Drain's house that night?
A. Yes.

SIGNED: (X) FRANK AGUILAR

(Signatures witnessed by Roy Montgomery, Roy Best, Arthur G. Wilson, J. Lee Sterling, W. L. McDonald, and E. C. Horne.)

Signed:
Joe Arridy

(editor's note: Aguilar signed with an "X" and his signature was witnessed by Roy Montgomery, prison guard. Asked if he would sign the statement also, Arridy agreed, signing his name with the spelling "Arrdy.")

Interestingly, Joe's signature appeared on the margin, all by itself and at the very end, with no formal witnesses following it. It seemed to be there almost as an afterthought. The interrogators nevertheless stated later that the document "will serve as the confession of both men" (Osborne, 1936).

❏ ❏ ❏

While Aguilar was being interrogated, Joe was brought before the two women who had been attacked in Pueblo earlier on the night of Dorothy Drain's murder. Both had been attacked from behind, with their arms forcefully pinioned to their sides. Earlier they had failed to identify Aguilar because they claimed they never saw him. After coming face to face with Joe, "The two women could not identify Arridy positively, although both said they believed their attacker was a man who resembled Arridy in some respect" (TPC, 10/3).

Another of Joe's confessions bites the dust. But the confession of his involvement in the murder of Dorothy Drain was going to stick.

20

POLITICAL FLUTTERS

On Thursday, August 27, when Joe Arridy's Cheyenne statement hit the papers, the Colorado governor rifled a telegram to institutional superintendent Jefferson:

DR B L JEFFERSON=
PLEASE MAKE FULL REPORT ARRIBY CASE WHY WERE PUEBLO PEACE OFFICERS NOT NOTIFIED WHY WAS THIS PERVERT WHO WAS NOT ADAPTED TO TRAINING IN THIS SCHOOL NOT TRANSFERRED TO PUEBLO ASYLUM AS ORDERED BY ME MONTHS AGO IN MY GENERAL ORDER TO TRANSFER SUCH CASES TO PUEBLO HAVE YOU ANY MORE DANGEROUS PERSONS IN YOUR SCHOOL WHO SHOULD HAVE CLOSER SUPERVISION THAN YOU ARE EQUIPPED TO GIVE=
    E. C. JOHNSON GOVERNOR

When I found this telegram in Governor Ed Johnson's files, I was surprised to find that a duplicate of the telegram had been sent to *The Denver Post*. I also found that superintendent Jefferson had responded with a telegram on the same day—from Pueblo (CSA, 1936):

GOVERNOR E C JOHNSON=
SHALL RENDER YOU FULL REPORT ARRIBY CASE ALSO YOUR QUESTIONS ASKED I CAME HERE FOR PURPOSE OF GIVING ASSISTANCE TO AUTHORITIES WHOM HAVE CASE IN CHARGE ON THE EVENING OF AUGUST THE EIGHTH AT WHICH TIME THE BOY RAN AWAY IMMEDIATE STEPS WERE TAKEN THROUGH THE SHERIFFS OFFICE AND POLICE OF GRAND JUNCTION AND MY PERSONAL EFFORTS IN MAKING A DILIGENT SEARCH FOR THIS BOY AND OTHERS WHO RAN AWAY IN NOT BEING SUCCESSFUL IN APPREHENDING THE BOY AND HIS COMPANION ADVICES WERE SENT ON AUGUST TENTH NINETEEN THIRTY SIX TO THE JUDGE OF THE COUNTY COURT PUEBLO COLO QUOTE DEAR SIR I WISH TO ADVISE YOU THAT JOE ARRIDY AN INMATE OF THIS HOME RAN AWAY FROM THE INSTITUTION THE EIGHTH OF THIS MONTH WE HAVE NOTIFIED SHERIFF AND POLICE AND ALL ARE ON THE LOOK OUT FOR THE BOY HIS FATHER LIVES AT 1139 ROUTT STREET PUEBLO THE BOY RAN AWAY SEVERAL DAYS AGO AND RETURNED OF HIS OWN FREE WILL AT THAT TIME I SENT WORD TO HIS FATHER SIGNED HELEN D COVER RN MATRON END QUOTE DESIRE TO SAY THE BOY REPORTED AS HAVING RUN AWAY WITH THE ARRIDY BOY I NOW HAVE IN JAIL AT HOT-SULPHURSPRINGS HE WILL BE QUES-

TIONED BY ME AS TO WHETHER HE AND THE ARRIDY BOY WERE IN PUEBLO OR
OTHER PLACES TOGETHER=
    B L JEFFERSON

As for Governor Johnson's asking why "this pervert" was not transferred to the
Colorado State Hospital according to his order, that request was made a year earlier, on
September 27, 1935. Superintendent Jefferson had responded three days later with a list
of nineteen residents, along with their diagnoses—including epileptic psychosis, dementia
praecox, insanity, juvenile insanity, and manic depressive phases. Joe Arridy's name was
not on the list.

On September 10, 1936, Superintendent Jefferson's "full" report was mailed to the
governor. It included many of the facts gleaned from Joe's institutional record—IQ 46, his
kitchen capabilities (tasks of not too long duration, can wash dishes, do mopping floors,
small chores and errands . . . depends on others for leadership). Jefferson mentioned that
Joe had perverse sexual habits—beginning with masturbation. But he stated that Joe had
never shown any sexual attraction for the female sex. Jefferson also included a full report
of the tracing of the runaways between August 8 and 13, carried out by himself and Val
Higgins.

Then came his first attempt to protect Joe. He pointed out that although Joe had reached
the age of 22, psychologically he was still a child "in children's clothes."

> An intelligent criminal avoids detection. It is to be remembered that the Mental Defectives
> are far more likely to be apprehended than the more intelligent law-breakers and taking it all
> around, their criminal activities are more accidental than planned intentionally.
>
> The Mental Defective may not know the difference between right or wrong; either through
> lack of appreciation of values, inability to profit by experience and remember the conse-
> quences, or the Moral Code.
>
> If Mental Defectives get into wrong company or form wrong habits, the feeble-minded
> scarcely ever get into the clutches of the Law until an adverse situation arises through
> directions or suggestion, they have not judgment (CSA, 1936).

Having said that, the report ended. Then Dr. Jefferson put in a good word for himself:

> When I first came to this Institution many things were needed; no one seemed to under-
> stand behavior problems of Mental Defectives by night and day. I ordered all of the Attendants
> to check up on every individual in the Home. Also, I have changed the Dormitory system; the
> construction of the buildings; everything to improve conditions for both Inmates and Em-
> ployees. I have given of my time . . . 24 hours a day . . . since I took charge of the Home.
>
> As to Psychological Classification, I have given study to each individual case; in this
> connection it should be remembered that the child may have a Neurosis or even a Psychosis
> and the conditions may produce conduct disorders which show a moral obliquity. I hope that
> this will satisfy you as to whether or not I have, in any manner, been careless or derelict in
> my duties.
>
> In conclusion, I wish to add that I assume full responsibility for Supervision of this
> Institution. I do not wish any blame to be attached to you, as Governor, or to the three
> Honorable Members of the Board of this Institution. If you desire any further information I

shall be pleased to furnish it.
I am Sir,
Respectfully,
B. L. Jefferson, M.D. (CSA, 1936)

Dr. Jefferson got the local sheriff to put in a good word for him, too:

To His Excellency Governor Johnson
Dear Governor:
Just a few lines regarding Dr. Jefferson and his trouble, there has been papers regarding Arridy case. Just wanted to say, Dr. Jefferson has always given us a ring whenever any of the boys or girls stray away and we of course have always confined our efforts in a radius of our County-Debeque, Mack, Palisades &c. and always had good luck in picking them up.

Last year I think it was three boys got as far as Salida and as I had a trip to Canon City, I picked them up and brought them home, they went away with a circus. On the 8th. instant Coles Circus was here and Dr. Jefferson came to the Sheriff's Office and asked our cooperation. My Under Sheriff and I went to the Circus manager and asked them to be sure and not allow any boys go to work or ride their trains out and this man called two of his head men and gave them orders not to hire any help in Grand Junction so we kept our eyes on the circus train and in the evening Dr. Jefferson reported that six of the boys are gone, we covered the train that night after it was made up but boys took an east-bound train. We never have wired out of our County as usually we get calls to us on these nuts.
Hoping that you will look at this as it really is,
I remain your friend,
Sheriff Charles S. Lumley (CSA, 1936)

Board President Val Higgins made a statement that triggered an emotional story in the September 2 edition of *The Daily Sentinel* in Grand Junction. The headline: PEOPLE OF COLORADO BLAMED FOR IMBECILES RUNNING LOOSE. It spoke out for the institution, but it didn't do much for Joe. The article:

There are 3,000 imbeciles in Colorado. Only 500 of them are confined in the institutions at Ridge and at Grand Junction. The state has no room for more and the legislature has not seen fit to provide for their care. Some of them are dangerous criminals and some of them are sex perverts. Every community is afflicted with a few of the criminal or pervert type.

Hundreds of them are hidden in homes under the watchful care of loving relatives, most of whom would gladly relinquish them to the state if they could be properly cared for.

These are the statements made by Val Higgins, city chaplain of the city of Denver, and member of the state board of control of the state eleemosynary institutions. . . .

"The people of Colorado do not realize the condition in this state," said Mr. Higgins. "We have tried repeatedly to secure money from the legislature for buildings for these unfortunates, but without success. There are 3,000 of them in the state. Nearly all of them are harmless, but a few are criminally inclined and some are sex perverts. They are to be distinguished from the insane, who are people that had mature minds, but lost their reason. These imbeciles are like babies or young children, either totally helpless or partially so.

"I did not realize conditions until I was placed on the board and I was amazed when professional men came to me and related that they were keeping their imbecile children locked in their own homes. Nobody suspected the existence of the imbecile in the family. They wanted the state to take care of them but we have room for only a small part" (TDS, 9-2-36).

Governor Ed Johnson got the message. On September 10, he signed an emergency executive order, appropriating $50,000 for aiding the expansion and improvement of homes for mental defectives, at both Grand Junction and Ridge (CSA, 1936).

In the meantime, Frank Aguilar prepared to go to trial and fight for his life. As for Joe Arridy's preparations, he didn't give a rip.

21

NATIONAL PURITY

While "The People of the State of Colorado" proceeded to cleanse their society of "subhuman" types like Frank Aguilar and Joe Arridy, another country went into the racial and intelligence purifying business big time. The Germans took the imperatives of the American eugenicists and statesmen—Henry Goddard, Madison Grant, Harry Laughlin, Henry Cabot Lodge, Chief Justice Oliver Wendell Holmes—and ran with them. They didn't fumble around with them like a bumbling democracy had. They just did them.

On July 14, 1933, Germany put into force its *Hereditary Health Law*. It was modeled after the law Henry Laughlin developed for Virginia—the one the U.S. Supreme Court upheld in 1927 and Oliver Wendell Holmes trumpeted to the world. "Three generations of imbeciles are enough." Hereditary health courts were set up across Germany to decide who had rotten genes and who didn't. By the end of the first year alone, more than 56,000 were sterilized, and many American eugenicists heralded this bold German move as leading-edge thinking and action (Smith, 1985, p. 154-55). So much for the "imbeciles," but what about "subhumans"? On September 15, 1935, the Germans mandated *The Law for the Protection of German Blood and Honor:*

> Imbued with the knowledge that the purity of German blood is the necessary prerequisite for the existence of the German nation, and inspired by an inflexible will to maintain the existence of the German nation for all future times, the Reichstag has unanimously adopted the following law which is now enacted:
>
> Article 1. (1) Any marriages between Jews and citizens of German or kindred blood are herewith forbidden. Marriages entered into despite this law are invalid, even if they are arranged abroad as a means of circumventing the law. . . .
>
> Article 2. Extramarital relations between Jews and citizens of German or kindred blood are herewith forbidden.
>
> Article 3. Jews are forbidden to employ as servants in their households female subjects of German or kindred blood who are under the age of forty-five years.
>
> Article 4. Jews are prohibited from displaying the Reich and national flag and from showing the national colors. . . .

And so it went for three more articles—articles that describe the boilerplate needed to keep the law strong and in force. Lest people think that Germany dreamed up this act of *rassenhygiene* all by themselves, they only need to consult *Virginia's Act to Preserve Racial*

Integrity of 1924 and see similar language prohibiting the marriage of white Americans and African Americans.

So in 1936, when criminal charges against Frank Aguilar and Joe Arridy were to some degree reinforced by their racial and intellectual backgrounds, Nordic-influenced eugenicists were on the move. In 1936, Harry Laughlin was awarded an honorary Doctor of Medicine degree from Nazi-controlled University of Heidelberg.

In 1936, the book of Nobel-Prize-winning Frenchman Alexis Carrel, *Man, the Unknown*, became a bestseller in the United States. He suggested that the human species might well consider killing off its worst types. He shared Germany's belief in the superiority of the Nordic race. His rationale: Nordic brains and nervous systems had not been so badly damaged by the hot sun:

> We must not forget that the most highly civilized races—the Scandinavians, for example—are white, and have lived for many generations in a country where the atmospheric luminosity is weak during a great part of the year. In France, the populations of the north are far superior to those of the Mediterranean shores. The lower races generally inhabit countries where light is violent and temperature equal and warm. It seems that the adaptation of white men to light and to heat takes place at the expense of their nervous and mental development (p. 214). . . .
>
> Florida and the French Riviera are suitable for weaklings, invalids, and old people, or normal individuals in need of a short rest. Moral energy, nervous equilibrium, and organic resistance are increased in children when they are trained to withstand heat and cold, dryness and humidity, burning sun and chilling rain, blizzards and fog—in short, the rigors of the seasons in northern countries (p. 304).

Small wonder that one of Carrel's closest friends was a tall, thin, light-skinned, blue-eyed Swede named Charles Lindbergh. And although Lindy was somewhat more careful with his statements, his once strong belief in the supremacy of Nazi Germany and his disgust for displaced persons—Russians, Poles, Slavs, and a few surviving Jews—may well have been spawned from long conversations with Carrel (Moseley, 1976, p. 333).

It was 1936, during the Berlin Olympics, and Adolph Hitler was sure that Nordic supremacy would prevail. Hitler announced that he would publicly honor the winners. But when the United States arrived with a cadre of athletes that included both Jews and African Americans, things became somewhat strained:

> When Hans Woelke won the shotput on opening day, Hitler had the first German champion of any Olympics paraded before him. But when [Jesse] Owens and his 'black auxiliaries,' as Hitler called them, exploded on the scene, it was a far different matter.
>
> Owens ran the 100 meters in a record 10.2 seconds, but it was disallowed because of a following wind. Other Negroes dominated their events. This put the Fuhrer on the spot. Hitler, who had congratulated other Olympic victors publicly, was faced with a dilemma. . . .
>
> His solution was to leave the stadium hastily, ostensibly because of threatening rain and the lateness of the hour. Hitler congratulated no other Olympic champions publicly. When Germans finished one-two in the hammer throw, he received them under the stands. Even when Lutz Long finished second to Owens in the broad jump, Hitler congratulated him privately and ignored Owens completely.
>
> But when Owens completed his triumphal performance at the Olympics by winning the 200-meter race in a record 20.7 seconds . . . Hitler again had left the stadium (Daniel, 1987).

In 1936, the United States was five years from entering World War II, and many Americans still saw Nazi Germany's pursuit of a pure society as a most attractive way to go.

In 1936, when Dorothy Drain was murdered, it also became a bad year for a Mexican national and a Syrian American in the United States.

22

AGUILAR TRIAL

A ROMAN HOLIDAY was the motivating thought yesterday of spectators who jammed the district courtroom where Frank Aguilar is on trial for his life. Barred from the room during the noonday recess, the spectators filled the hall and lined up in impatient expectation until the doors were opened for the afternoon session. Then, like a bunch of school boys tearing out of school with the last bell, like happy children at an Easter egg roll, like striking Communists in Paris, or the five o'clock subway rush in New York, they burst into the court room, each intent upon being the first to get a seat. This photograph shows them in the act of bursting. Notice the triumphant expression on the faces of those who already have gained seats for Pueblo's trial of the decade; notice the elbowing and pushing among those trying to get thru the door; notice, too, that there are more people already in than the court will hold, and that many will have to stand. . . .

So went the caption below the front-page photograph taken before a court session began (TPC, Dec. 17). When District Judge William B. Stewart took his seat at the bench, he made it plain to the unruly audience that a holy test for truth was about to be carried out in this court, and he would allow nothing to mess it up. He also made it plain that the audience could laugh "only when the court does—which will be not at all."

Unfortunately, I never found any trial transcripts from *The People v. Frank Aguilar*. County clerks doubted if they still existed. But many of the key parts survived, thanks to *The Pueblo Chieftain*. They obviously hired their own court reporter and filled page after page with transcripts from the trial—especially those passages on which the trial turned.

TUESDAY, DECEMBER 15

Court testimony began exactly three months after the crime. The day opened with more or less uninteresting testimony by medical experts, but the day ended in a smashing climax when Riley A. Drain, Dorothy's father, took the stand. Drain testified that he, his daughter Barbara, and others had obtained a second confession—an oral one—at the Canon City penitentiary (TPC, 12-14).

The father began his testimony by describing what he found after coming home from the dance. He paused in the telling repeatedly when he became emotionally overwhelmed. He then testified that Aguilar had worked for him for seven months on a WPA project.

He talked about his various contacts with the man—one in which he and Aguilar were in the yard together at the Drain home. He said that Aguilar knew both girls. Then Prosecutor Taylor asked, "Where did you next see the defendant?":

A. At the penitentiary.
Q. When?
A. November 27, 1936.
Q. When you first saw him, who were present?
A. French L. Taylor, Roy Best, Barbara Drain, another fellow I didn't know, and myself.
Q. Did you have any conversation with the defendant?
A. Yes.
Q. Did you have any conversation to do with the murder of your daughter, Dorothy Drain?
A. Yes, it all had to do with the murder.
Q. You will please state what that conversation was.

With that, defense attorney Vasco G. Seavy was on his feet. He objected, saying that the proper foundation for the confession had not been laid. Judge Stewart sustained the objection and ordered the jury removed until he ruled on the confession's admissibility. Then, without the jury, Drain continued: "I asked him to tell me about this thing, and how he did it. I told him I was the one he should have told, not somebody else."

According to Drain, Aguilar described what happened on the night of the crime. He was on Northern avenue, started to go to a show, changed his mind, and bought half a pint of whiskey. Later, he said it must have been muscatel wine. He said he was drunk and that he went home and lay down. Later, when a man came to inquire about some money Aguilar owed, Aguilar went with him back to Northern avenue. And there he met—Joe Arridy. Shortly after that statement, the court recessed for the day.

WEDNESDAY

It was a bitter session. Without the jury present, the defense spent the whole day arguing vehemently that the confession Aguilar gave Drain should be excluded, because physical violence and threats were employed in forcing him to say what his interrogators wanted to hear. Aguilar testified that he was home asleep by eight o'clock on the night of the crime. Then defense attorney Seavy asked about the happenings on November 27.

Q. Did you tell Mr. Drain at the time that you had murdered his daughter?
A. Yes, I did.
Q. Had you murdered his daughter?
A. No.
Q. Why did you tell him that, then?
A. Because Mr. Roy Best was there.
Q. Why did the fact that Roy Best was there cause you to tell Drain what you did?
A. Because he [Best] said to me he was going to my cell that night, that he would be the only one there, and that he was going to make me suffer just the same as I did Mr. Drain's daughters.
Q. What effect did that have on you?
A. I thought he was really going to do it.

Aguilar said that two of the prison officers called him names, and Best had said that "in 15 minutes there would be a dead Mexican " (TPC, 12-17). Best and other officers took the stand and denied such assertions. Best declared that he never interfered in cases that were not his.

THURSDAY

Judge Stewart ruled that the confession was admissible. With the jury present, Riley Drain once more described what Aguilar had said he did during the hours before the crime. This time the story was more complete and presented with greater detail. He reached the point at which Aguilar told him about going with the man to whom he owed money:

> I said, "Well, when did you meet Arridy?"
> He said, "Not then."
> I said, "Well, when *did* you meet Arridy?"
> He said, "Later. I saw Arridy in Bessemer park, and we went home and got this ax—or hatchet, whatever it was—and we went to my [Drain's] house and watched thru the back window till he saw me [Drain] leave with my wife."

Drain then had asked a number of pointed questions about going into the house and into the girls' room, which Aguilar dodged with "You ought to know" and "I don't remember." Then Drain asked the tough questions:

> I said, "Did you ravish Dorothy?"
> He said, "Yes."
> I said, "Did Arridy ravish Barbara?"
> Drain momentarily buried his face in his left hand at that point and, showing strong emotion, talked with considerable hesitation.
> *He said he didn't know, as he went out* (author's emphasis).

Later, Prosecutor Taylor asked Drain, "State whether or not at any time during his conversation, he told you who hit Barbara or Dorothy." Seavy objected on the grounds that the question was leading and suggestive. Judge Steward upheld the objection.

> Questioned by Taylor: "Have you told me all he said about striking the girls or either of them?"
> A. "I can't remember now what he said about that."

For most of the remaining time, defender Seavy vigorously cross-examined Drain. Most of his questions were attempts to show the jury that Aguilar's statements to Drain were not voluntary and that the prosecutor may have put certain statements into the witness's mouth.

FRIDAY

It was a heavy-evidence day, with Detective Horne on the stand. He identified the head of the hatchet, a shirt worn by Aguilar with blood on its sleeve, and some bloody sheets.

(A coverlet on the bed had been admitted as evidence the day before.) Three confessions were described by Horne—the one given to Drain, an oral confession Aguilar made at Canon City, and the written one that followed.

During cross-examination, Seavy asked Horne to describe his trip to Cheyenne after Chief Carroll's first call. Then Seavy's questions focused on Joe:

Q. Your impression of Arridy was that he was a mentally defective, an irresponsible person?
A. That's correct.
Q. With very little intelligence?
A. Very little.
Q. Hardly a good smart child?
A. Yes.
   [Later]
Q. Prior to being called to Cheyenne, you had certain theories, and after Arridy came into the case, you changed these theories. Is that right?
A. No, we followed the same theories we had had about the case—we always figured it was a one-man job.
Q. In all your experience as a police officer, did you ever hear of a crime of this kind being a two-man job?
A. This is the only one.
Q. But on the statement of a half-wit, you changed to make it a two-man job?
   [Talking at length, Horne finally agreed that the two men then became connected to the same crime.]
Q. After Arridy had told you folks a story, you then began to confront Aguilar with what Arridy had said, didn't you?
A. We did on September 2.

As the day ended, all the confessions were being hotly contested by Seavy (TPC, 12-19).

SATURDAY

Judge Stewart ordered the weekend session. The trial was moving well, and he wasn't about to slow down the pace. And here, one more bombshell threatened to blow a hole in Seavy's defense.

Dr. Frances McConnell, a toxicologist from Denver, claimed that scrapings from under the fingernails of Aguilar contained fibers from the coverlet on the girls' bed. She also testified that a single hair from the crime scene matched a hair taken from Joe Arridy. McConnell was on the staff of several Denver hospitals, and at the present time was doing serious lab work on hay-fever allergies and the cause of the common cold. Even so, she claimed that her sporadic lab work for court cases was carried out with extreme care and exactness.

Seavy jumped with both feet into questions about how the hair and fibers were taken by the detectives, stored in a box in a heavily trafficked room, then ultimately delivered to Dr. McConnell in Denver on August 26 (at about the same time Sheriff Carroll was beginning his interrogation of Joe).

MONDAY

Judge Stewart began by overruling the defense motion to strike the confessions. Taylor called Detective McDonald to the stand, who repeated and reinforced much of Detective Horne's earlier testimony. Seavy was relentless in his cross-examination. Then Dr. O'Connell took the stand for additional cross-examination.

But somehow all that was said must have grown dim in the jury's minds after Taylor called his last witness for the prosecution—Barbara Drain. Taylor slowly and carefully delivered his foundation questions about going to sleep on the night of the crime. Then came the crucial query:

Q. When you woke up, what, if anything, did you see?
A. I saw the face of a man.
Q. What did you say, if anything?
A. Well, I thought he was my daddy at first, and I didn't say anything.
Q. After that, did you say anything to him?
A. I told him to get out.
Q. Did you realize at any time that he wasn't your daddy?
A. Yes sir.
Q. After you realized he wasn't your daddy, what did you say?
A. I told him to get out.
Q. Where was he standing when you saw him?
A. He was inside the door.
Q. What happened next?
A. I don't remember anything after that.
Q. When he stood there and you saw him, did you get a view of his face? I mean the front or side of the face?
A. I got a view of the side of his face.
Q. Since coming to this courtroom, have you seen that man?
A. Yes sir.
Q. Have you seen him today?
A. Yes (TPC, 12-22).

Barbara was asked to take Taylor to the man. A reporter described the scene:

Then the little witness, victim of the same attack that killed her sister, walked across the room at the request of District Attorney French Taylor, and stood in front of Frank Aguilar. She pointed to him as the man she saw in her bedroom on the night of Aug. 15. It was a dramatic moment, and the courtroom was tense as it was enacted. Then, Barbara's testimony completed, the state rested its case (TPC, 12-22).

Seavy's cross-examination was tender and short. He did not question her identification of the defendant, and after that, the defense slowly unraveled.

After Aguilar's mother testified for the defense that her son was home on the night of the crime, the judge called an emergency recess so that the jury could get some fresh air—an attempt to keep them from falling asleep. That evening, the unraveling continued:

Monday night, it was reliably reported, Aguilar for the first time admitted to Vasco G. Seavy, his attorney, that he had committed the crime. Previously he had always denied participating in the crime and claimed that the confessions he gave officers were forced from him.

Upon receiving the admission, Seavy, it is understood, at once sought out officers of the Bar Association, laying the situation before them. Tuesday morning, they conferred with Judge Stewart. Under the law, an attorney is bound by his client's wishes (TPC, 12-23).

TUESDAY, DECEMBER 22

Judge Stewart called a recess until 2:00 P.M. At that time, defender Seavy asked the court to substitute a plea of "not guilty by reason of insanity" in place of the original not-guilty plea—Denied.

Seavy asked for an adjournment to marshal new facts in order to secure a new defense—Denied.

Seavy's original plan to call the defendant and his wife for the purpose of establishing an alibi was scrapped, and the case went to the jury without further argument.

The jury found Frank Aguilar guilty.

❏ ❏ ❏

A few minutes after the verdict, Aguilar was placed in the custody of Pueblo County Sheriff Lewis Worker and Warden Roy Best. Handcuffed to prison guard Roy Montgomery, he started on his way to Canon City.

Mrs. R. O. McMurtree attended the trial on that final Tuesday. She and her aunt, Sally Crumpley, had been sleeping in their bed two weeks before the Drain murder, when an attacker entered the room and beat both of them about the head with a hammer, killing Mrs. Crumpley. As Aguilar was being taken away, she named him as her assailant.

❏ ❏ ❏

Aguilar's trial was over, and Joe Arridy's would soon begin. And now there were many facts and questions that would need to be handled anew.

Joe was never present at Aguilar's trial. It was repeatedly implied that he was not competent to be a witness. And yet, didn't the prosecutors use Joe *in absentia*? Did they not use Joe's confession in one of their attempts to connect Aguilar to the Drain murder? Did they not consider that his confession was competently given?

Joe allegedly was connected with Aguilar on the night of the crime. He was placed in the Drain home at the time of the crime. But was he? And what did he really do? Why did Barbara fail to mention Joe when she identified Aguilar?

Dr. O'Connell claimed that one single hair which the detectives picked up from the bedding at the crime scene matched Joe's hair. What will happen when she brings that single hair to Joe's trial?

23

SANITY TRIAL

Today we claim that defendants are not competent to stand trial: (1) if they cannot assist their attorneys in the preparation of their cases; (2) if they do not understand the court proceedings; and (3) if they do not understand the punishment. Two national experts have even developed a test for determining whether people like Joe Arridy are truly competent to stand trial at all (Everington and Luckasson, 1992).

In Joe Arridy's day, there were no standards like that. The only way court-appointed defense attorney C. Fred Barnard could save his client's life was to convince a jury that he was insane. So on October 31, 1936, Barnard told the court that Joe was "not guilty by reason of insanity." Upon hearing this, the judge ordered Joe to be taken from the penitentiary and committed to the Colorado State Hospital in Pueblo. The judge appointed three of the hospital's psychiatrists—Superintendent F. H. Zimmerman, J. L. Rosenblum, and Paul S. Wolf —"to observe and examine" Joe's mental condition and report their findings at the sanity trial (*People v Arddy*, #24733. District Court, Pueblo County, Colorado, 10/36).

On Monday, February 8, 1937, Joe's sanity trial began. Early in the trial, Judge Harry Leddy made it clear that the jury should answer only one question: Does Joe Arridy "have the capacity to tell good from evil and right from wrong?" If he wasn't able to tell the difference, the jury should rule him insane, and he would be remanded to either the institution in Pueblo or the one at Grand Junction. If he were voted sane, another jury must decide whether he was guilty or innocent of the murder of Dorothy Drain (*People v Arrdy*, p. 49).

Superintendent Zimmerman took the stand and testified that Joe was not capable of determining the difference between right and wrong. But being a psychiatrist full of the latest theories, he had a hard time saying that Joe was insane. He claimed that a person had to be healthy-minded before going insane.

According to Zimmerman, Joe had never had a healthy mind. He possessed a child's mind in a man's body, and he had always been that way. Like a child, he was very susceptible to suggestions from others. Zimmerman said that Joe was intelligent enough to identify a penny, a nickel, a dime, a quarter, and a half-dollar, but he hesitated in identifying the last two coins. He said that Joe was "just a little above the idiot phase."

[By Defender Barnard]: Dr. Zimmerman, you stated Joe was just a little above the idiot phase, more of an imbecile. Will you explain, Doctor, what the idiot and imbecile are, if you can?

A. For practical purposes we classify all individuals whose mentality is less than the five-year level as idiots; from the five-year level to the nine, we feel that they are imbeciles. I am speaking of adults who are afflicted with mental defects. And then above that, from the ninth- to the twelve-year level into the moron grade. Above that, you get into your normals.

Q. You say he is above the idiot; you mean about six years old?

A. About that. In some ways he may be a little above the six year old; in others, a little less than a six year old (p. 55).

Dr. Rosenblum added to Zimmerman's view of Joe by testifying that he "could count up to five; maybe up to ten," but it was more mechanical than intellectual. As for being able to tell right from wrong, "It must be a very vague, misty sort of impression, which would not, in my opinion, be at all consistent with the same knowledge an adult normally would have."

During cross-examination, Prosecutor Ralph J. Neary allowed Rosenblum to soar to his esoteric best—on how environment affects intelligence, why in some cultures polygamy is right and in others it is wrong, how one is taught right from wrong. Then Neary slowly and deftly brought Rosenblum down to Joe's situation:

Q. In other words, a person's conception of right and wrong is based upon environment, and their teachings?

A. Very largely.

Q. [Motioning toward Joe Arridy] You are not saying that this man is insane, are you?

A. No, I wouldn't say he was insane, because you have heard the definition given a few minutes ago, which summarizes the difference between mental idiocy *per se* or mental deficiency. The normal man is born with a full supply of intelligence. Misfortune overcame him, and he becomes insane. The mental defective has been illy equipped from birth (p. 81).

Dr. Wolf took the stand and repeated the same observations and theories about Joe being a little bit above the idiot stage, and—like the other psychiatrists—stated that "he is not insane, he is in the imbecile class." By the time prosecutor Neary cross-examined Dr. Wolf, the audience was responding with smiles and muffled laughter.

[Prosecutor Neary]: Does he appreciate the connection between the means and the end; that is, the end of his thought and the means of attaining it?

[Dr. Wolf]: About the best he can do in that is to imitate what he sees somebody do in a very similar manner. For instance, if he sees me a number of times use a mop, he can use the mop, too.

Q. Would you say that same thing in regard to sexual intercourse?

A. I imagine he was initiated.

Q. Doctor, you classified him between five or six years of age?

A. Yes sir.

Q. Would you say a boy of five or six years of age would climb on a freight train after having assaulted a girl, and then go to Cheyenne?

A. He probably ran up to a freight car as a place to hide, and it took him to Cheyenne accidentally; he didn't know where he was going.

Q. In other words, if he did that for the purpose of going to Cheyenne, he would have had to see somebody else do that two or three times before he would do it?
[The audience in the court room breaks out in laughter.]
THE COURT: We are very glad to have the public here if they want to listen to the trial, but they must be quiet, and that means everybody.
A. You see, he didn't plan to go to Cheyenne. He had probably seen other people get on boxcars before he did that. He did that, but he didn't know where the boxcar was going. It happened to go to Cheyenne (p. 68-69).

Prosecutor Neary must have known he was on a roll. He must have known that the longer he let Dr. Wolf mesh his educated theories with his observations of Joe, the more disgusted the courtroom audience would become. He stayed on Wolf:

[Prosecutor Neary]: Doctor, when you talked to Joe Arridy, was his attention concentrated on what you were saying?
[Dr. Wolf]: Not always.
Q. What is his concentration?
A. It is very loosely organized; it varies so much; he is easily distracted, even more so, I think, than a child of his mental age.
Q. In other words, his span of attention is less than a child of the mental age you have described in there?
A. Yes, it is.
Q. Have you noticed him sitting here during this trial?
A. Yes.
Q. Does he squirm and look around like a child of that age would do?
A. No matter how still he sits, his eyes move around; I have noticed him.
Q. But a child of the age of four to six would be squirming around or running around talking to someone, would he not?
A. Most children would; not all.

REDIRECT EXAMINATION

[Defender Bernard]: Would you say he understands what is going on?
[Dr. Wolf]: No, I wouldn't.
Q. Would you say he is concentrating on anything that is being said?
A. No, he has no concentrating powers at all; makes no effort to concentrate or digest it.
Q. Isn't it a fact, probably, that he doesn't know what is going on here today?
A. His mind is almost entirely a blank (pp. 71-72).

Even though the knowledge of right and wrong was the key issue, the audience—and possibly the jury—found it curious that the three psychiatrists could say that Joe was not insane at a trial trying to find whether he was in his right mind. *The Chieftain* amplified this dilemma in the next day's headlines.

ALIENISTS TESTIFY ARRIDY HAS MIND OF SIX-YEAR-OLD
STATE HOSPITAL PHYSICIANS TELL JURY BOY'S NOT INSANE—
JUST AN IMBECILE

❏ ❏ ❏

After the three psychiatric witnesses, Fred Barnard was supposed to rest the defense's case, but he didn't. Instead, he called Joe Arridy to the stand. *He suddenly decided to let Joe speak for himself!*

The court clerk told Joe to face him, place his left hand on the Bible, raise his right hand and answer, "Yes," after the clerk said, "Do you swear to tell the whole truth and nothing but the truth, so help you God?"

[By Mr. Barnard]:

Q. Joe, do you know what an oath is?

A. No.

Q. Do you know what this man is speaking to you here (indicating Clerk of the Court)?

A. I don't think so.

Q. What did he say to you; do you know what he said to you?

A. No.

Q. How old are you, Joe?

A. I am about twenty-two.

Q. What is your name?

A. Joe.

Q. Joe what?

A. Joe Arddy.

A. Joe, have you ever been in the Home for the Feeble Minded at Grand Junction?

A. Yes.

Q. When did you get out of there?

A. I don't know.

Q. How long ago was it?

A. It is about three or four months.

Q. Did you run away?

A. Yes.

Q. Where were you going?

A. Going to Denver and Pueblo and Cheyenne.

Q. Joe, who is Franklin Delano Roosevelt? Do you know who he is?

A. I don't guess I know.

Q. Do you know who George Washington was? Have you ever heard of George Washington?

A. No.

Q. Well, who is the president of the United States, Joe?

A. Hoover.

Q. Hoover? Who is Franklin Roosevelt?

(No answer)

Q. What are we doing?

A. Trial.

Q. What kind of trial? On what? Do you know what the hearing is about?

A. No.

CROSS-EXAMINATION

[By Mr. Neary]:
Q. Do you know Dorothy Drain?
A. No I don't.
Q. Did you ever know her?
A. No.
Q. Do you know these officers?
A. I don't think so.
Q. You never saw them before?
A. No.
Q. Do you know your father?
A. Yes.
Q. Where is your mother?
A. Home.
Q. Where is your father?
A. Home.
Q. Your father is home, is that right, Joe?
A. Yes.
Q. Isn't that your father there? (indicating)
A. Uh-huh.
Q. He isn't home then, is he?
A. No.
Q. Do you know Frank?
A. No.
Q. Do you know Frank Aguilar?
A. I don't know him.
Q. Do you remember what you did when you got out of the home over at Grand Junction?
A. Catch freight train.
Q. Where were you going? Where did you go?
A. Pueblo, Denver, and Cheyenne.
Q. Did you go to Pueblo?
A. Yes sir.
Q. What did you do there?
A. Nothing.
Q. What did you do in Denver?
A. Find job.
Q. What did you do in Colorado Springs?
A. I find a job.
Q. What did you do in Cheyenne?
A. Loafing around.
Q. You didn't do anything in Pueblo?
A. No.
Q. Do you know Dr. Zimmerman?
A. Yes.
Q. Do you know Dr. Wolf?
A. Yes.
Q. Do you know Dr. Rosenblum?

A. Yes.

Q. Where are they?

A. State Hospital.

Q. Did you see them today?

A. Yes.

Q. What were they doing here today?

A. Talking.

Q. Talking about what?

A. Talking about me.

Q. What about you?

A. Oh, about something.

Q. Don't you know what they were talking about?

A. No, forgot.

Q. Can you tell me anything they talked about?

A. I don't think so.

Q. You don't know Dorothy Drain?

A. No.

Q. Never heard of her?

A. No.

Q. You don't know any of these men here at all?

A. I don't think so.

Q. Never saw them?

A. No.

Q. Do you know what I am doing here?

A. No.

Q. Do you know Mr. Barnard?

A. Yes. [He looks at Mr. Barnard and smiles (TPC, 2-9)]

Q. What is he doing here?

A. Sitting.

Q. Is he doing anything else here today?

A. Yes, talking.

Q. Who is he talking about?

A. About me.

Q. Where have you been; where did you come from today?

A. State Hospital.

Q. How long have you been there?

A. I guess about sixty days. [Actually, more than 90 days. He was admitted for observation on October 31, 1936]

Q. You say your name is Joe Arrdy?

A. Yes.

Q. (Handing blank paper) Will you write your name on there for me?
(Defendant's Exhibit A marked for identification)
MR. NEARY: We offer this in evidence, if Your Honor please.
MR. BERNARD: No objection.
THE COURT: It will be admitted.
Defendant's Exhibit A was passed to the jury.

Q. What did you do over in Grand Junction, Joe?

A. Working.

Q. What did you do?
A. Kitchen.
Q. What did you do in the kitchen?
A. I washed dishes.
Q. What else?
A. Everything.
Q. Did you go to school there?
A. Yes.
Q. What did you study?
A. Just a little.
Q. A little what?
A. Just a little; read a book.
Q. Can you read?
A. Not very good.
Q. (Showing a dime) Do you know what that is?
A. Ten.
Q. (Showing nickel) Do you know what that is?
A. Nickel.
Q. (Showing quarter) Do you know what that is?
A. Quarter.
Q. What color is my tie?
A. Red [Correct]
Q. What color is my suit?
A. Black [Dark blue]
Q. What color is your shirt?
A. Green [Light blue]
Q. Are you sure? Look at it.
A. Yes.
Q. What is that up there on the wall?
A. Clock. [He smiles (TPC)]
Q. What time is it?
A. Quarter till five. [Hesitated before answering. Actually, it was 20 minutes to five (TPC)]
Q. Where are you going tonight, Joe?
A. Back to Grand Junction.
Q. You are not going back to the State Hospital?
A. Huh-uh (no).
Q. Why are you going back to Grand Junction?
A. I like the place.
Q. You want to do what you like to do, don't you, Joe?
A. Yes.
Q. Do you like girls?
A. Pretty good. [He smiles again (TPC)]
Q. After you left Grand Junction did you come to Pueblo?
A. Yes.
Q. What did you see here?
A. I didn't see nobody.
Q. Didn't you see your mother?

A. Never was home.

Q. Did you see your father?

A. I can't find the home.

Q. And where did you go then?

A. Went back to Cheyenne and Denver.

Q. Did you stop in Colorado Springs?

A. Pretty near.

Q. Why didn't you stop?

A. Train stopped.

Q. What did you do?

A. Catch the next one.

Q. Did you go any place in Colorado Springs?

A. No.

Q. Where did you go when you got off the train?

A. Went to Cheyenne.

Q. Can you count, Joe?

A. A little.

Q. Count for the jury. Don't know how?

A. Not much.

Q. Can you say, "I am sleepy."

A. I am sleepy.

Q. Can you say, "I am tired and sleepy"?

A. I am tired and sleepy.

Q. Can you say, "I want to go back to Grand Junction because I like it better?"

A. I want to go back to Grand Junction, I like it better.

Q. Did you ever see a hatchet, Joe?

A. I don't think so.

Q. Never saw a hatchet?

A. Never saw a hatchet.

Q. Do you know what a hatchet is?

A. No.

Q. Do you know what a ditch is, irrigation ditch?

A. No.

Q. Do you know what bushes are?

A. Trees.

Q. Bushes, low trees?

A. Weeds.

Q. Do you know what weeds are?

A. Yes.

Q. Did you ever hide behind weeds?

A. No.

Q. You didn't hide behind any weeds in Colorado Springs?

A. No.

Q. Did you knock down a girl in Colorado Springs?

A. No.

Q. What happened? Do you remember?

A. Nothing.

Q. Nothing happened, you know that?

A. Uh-huh.

Q. Were you ever at the state penitentiary at Canon City?

A. Yes.

Q. When?

A. I guess about five days.

Q. About five days you were there? Do you remember hiding your shirt up in Wyoming?

A. No.

Q. You didn't hide your shirt in Wyoming; what did you do up there?

A. Try to find a job.

Q. If you tried to find a job, why do you want to back to Grand Junction? You like it better there?

A. Yes.

Q. Do you like it better in Grand Junction?

A. I like it better in Grand Junction.

Q. Why did you leave Grand Junction then?

A. Oh, some kids was bothering me.

Q. How did they bother you?

A. They just hit me.

Q. Who hit you?

A. Just fool kid.

Q. How many times?

A. About three or four times.

Q. Where did they hit you?

A. I guess all over.

Q. All over your face; did it hurt?

A. A little bit, not much.

Q. Is that why you left Grand Junction?

A. Yes.

Q. And now you would like to go back there?

A. Yes.

Q. Do you know that man standing there?

A. I know him, but can't tell you his name.

Q. Do you know him; where did you see him, Joe?

A. Down in jail.

Q. But you don't know any of the rest of these men here?

A. No.

Q. Never seen them; is that right?

A. Sure.

Q. Do you know any of these men on the jury?

A. No.

Q. Do you know this man, the stenographer?

A. No.

Q. Do you know that man (indicating Judge Leddy)?

A. No.

Q. Do you know what he is doing here?

A. Talking.

REDIRECT EXAMINATION

[By Mr. Barnard]:
Q. Joe, can you read?
A. Not very good.
Q. (Showing paper) Can you see that?
A. Yes.
Q. What does it say? What does it say? Do you know what it says?
A. No.
Q. Can you write?
A. Sure.
Q. Can you write anything besides your name?
A. My name.
    (THE COURT declared a recess until 10 o'clock A.M., Tuesday, February 9, 1937).
    MR. BARNARD: The Defense Rests
    (*The People v. Arddy* #24733. District Court, Pueblo County, Colorado. pp. 43-50)

❏ ❏ ❏

On Tuesday, February 9, 1937, the prosecution's case was relatively quick and crisp. The first witness was Detective W. L. McDonald. He talked briefly about the things he observed during the interrogations of Joe. Then prosecutor Neary maneuvered McDonald into answering the key question:

[By Prosecutor Neary]:
Q. You have had quite a lot of experience as a police officer, haven't you?
A. Yes, quite a little.
Q. How long?
A. Twenty-five years. In September.
Q. During those years as a police officer you have had an opportunity to contact many different types and characters of men?
A. I have.
Q. Based upon your experience as a police officer, dealing with these types of men, and your observation of Joe Arddy during the times you have mentioned, you may state, in your opinion whether or not Joe Arddy knows the difference between right and wrong, and knowing the difference between right and wrong, has he a mind of sufficient strength to follow the good and avoid the evil?
A. I think he has (pp. 88-89).
[Later, during cross-examination by Defender Barnard]:
Q. Mr. McDonald, you have testified previously as to the facts involved in this case, have you not?
A. I have.
Q. When was that?
A. Well, sometime in December; I think the trial started on the fourteenth [McDonald was referring to the Aguilar trial].
Q. Mr. McDonald, why at that time did you state that Joe Arrdy had the mentality of about a five- or six-year-old boy?
A. I don't ever remember saying that.

Q. If you did state that, would you say that statement was wrong?
A. No, I wouldn't.
Q. What do you think now with reference to his mental age?
A. I would say he was along about that, about five or six.
Q. Upon what do you base your opinion as to whether or not he knows the difference between right and wrong?
A. From the different details of the crime he related to us in Cheyenne (p. 90).
[Later. By Mr. Barnard]:
Q. He was powerfully subject to suggestion?
A. No. Nothing was ever suggested in my presence.
Q. Do you mean that police officers, sheriff's officers, going into a crime of that sort, act the part of gentlemen and never suggest anything?
A. I would always act the part of a gentleman.
Q. You would never try to force anybody to say anything?
A. Never (p. 90).
[Later. By Mr. Barnard]:
Q. Would you say the testimony of [the three psychiatrists] was absolutely wrong when they say that this boy cannot tell the difference between right and wrong?
A. I believe it was the last witness, Dr. Wolf, I listened very attentively to his testimony.
Q. Would you say his testimony was wrong?
A. Yes.
Q. What was that?
A. That the defendant as he sits in court, that his mind is a total blank.
Q. Would you say that, even after knowing that Dr. Wolf, with his medical knowledge and his knowledge of mental diseases, observed and examined this boy for thirty days, when you only examined him for a period of thirty minutes at one time; one hour again, and one hour again?
A. I would not discredit the doctor's testimony on anything; he is a learned man, as was evident in the courtroom yesterday. I would say the doctor was wrong at that particular time (p. 91).

The second officer on the stand was Detective Everett Horne. He moved through the same drill. Based on his fifteen years of police experience, he believed that Joe Arridy knew right from wrong. Defender Barnard, during cross-examination, recalled Horne testifying in the Aguilar trial that Joe had the capacity of a five-year-old child. Horne denied saying it. Barnard said he had said it. There were some awkward moments for Horne, but he moved through them.

[By Mr. Barnard]:
Q. What is your opinion now, Mr. Horne, of this man's mental age?
A. I haven't any opinion.
Q. Did you hear the testimony of the doctors yesterday?
A. I did.
Q. Would you say they were wrong when they said he was mentally between four and six?
A. I wouldn't care to argue with doctors on the question.
Q. Do you think you are as well qualified to express an opinion as to his ability to distinguish between right and wrong as these doctors?
A. After listening to them three doctors yesterday, I think we are all crazy (p. 95).

Then came a man with prestige, Colorado Springs Chief of Police Hugh D. Harper. He testified that he had been chief since 1917. Although he wasn't involved in the Drain case, he had interrogated Joe for "between one hour and two." This was occasioned by the woman in Colorado Springs who initially claimed that Joe had attacked her—at least until it was clear that her attacker had been seen in Cheyenne at the time of the crime. Based on his short visit with Joe and his years of experience, he was sure that Joe knew the difference between right and wrong.

The fourth and last witness for the prosecution was Cheyenne Sheriff George J. Carroll. His testimony was based on his "seven or eight" hours of interrogation with Joe:

[By Prosecutor Neary]:
Q. Did he recount to you the details of this alleged murder?
A. Yes, he did.
Q. Were those details right?
A. They checked out almost perfect.
Q. You may state, Sheriff, whether when you questioned Joe Arddy, were your questions based on suggestion, or not?
A. Well, I didn't know what to suggest, because I didn't know any of the details of the crime, and I questioned him for details in order to check up with the department here at Pueblo to see if they were correct.
Q. You didn't know what they were.
A. I just read the account in the newspaper, which didn't give details.
[Later, when Neary asked Carroll if Joe Arridy had the power to tell right from wrong]:
A. He exemplified that, and stated that he was very sorry for what had happened, so much so that he cried and shed copious tears (p. 102).

When it came to testifying, the four police officers beat the three psychiatrists, hands down. The officers were poised, spoke crisply, and though they may have been wrong sometimes—or lied—they never appeared to be in doubt. The psychiatrists, on the other hand, tried to defend Joe and also be faithful to their latest theories.

After pouring over the transcripts time and time again, *it was Joe Arridy's being allowed to speak for himself that touched me most and gave me a better understanding of the man.* I felt so strongly about this that I put every word he said into this chapter. Surely the jury would understand Joe better after he took the stand and spoke for himself.

But they didn't.

The case went to the jury at 2:30 P.M. By 9:00 P.M., the jury was deadlocked six to six. In less than an hour after that, a verdict was reached: The jury voted that Joe Arridy did know the difference between right and wrong. The jury considered him to be sane.

Joe was never again allowed to speak for himself in a courtroom, and he would now face a new jury—one that would decide whether he was guilty or innocent of the murder of Dorothy Drain. It would be a trial for his life.

24

THE BIG TRIAL

On Monday, April 12, 1937, *The People of the State of Colorado versus Joe Arddy*, case number 24733, began. The evidence and countering evidence had already been presented in the case against Frank Aguilar, who had been found guilty and sentenced to death. Now it was Joe's turn.

The Pueblo County District Court was packed, waiting to hear what the prosecution and the defense had to offer. So much had been printed in the newspapers about the case; now was the time to find out what was real and what was phony.

The trial began with an unprecedented bizarre twist.

Prosecutor Ralph J. Neary would present evidence of guilt as he usually does.

Defender E. Fred Barnard, however, would not present countering evidence. He would cross-examine the prosecution's witnesses, of course, but he would not put defense witnesses on the stand to try to refute, point-by-point, the prosecution's case. Instead, Barnard would call only the doctors as the defense witnesses. One more time, Barnard would try to convince a jury that Joe was insane.

After being peppered with technical exceptions and new motions by Barnard, Judge Harry Leddy set aside the earlier verdict that Joe was sane. He ruled that this big trial would now encompass guilt or innocence, as well as sanity or insanity (transcript pp. 1-3).

According to press reports and the transcript, another contradiction was present in the trial. Joe Arridy, a small, shy, always nonviolent man, was supposed to have been part of one of the town's most unspeakably violent acts. It was reported that he sat quietly in the courtroom—facing forward, almost frozen, never speaking. Even while he sat that way, Prosecutor Neary asked questions that moved witnesses to point to Joe as if he were the devil, and swear that, in spite of his soft, vacant passiveness, he knew everything that went on in the Drain home on the night of August 15, and he knew everything that was going on in the courtroom as well.

One more surprise was introduced as the trial opened: Defender Barnard asked the court's permission to postpone his opening statement. He asked that Neary be allowed to make his opening statement and present all the prosecution witnesses first. After the prosecution rested, Barnard would deliver his opening statement.

Prosecutor Neary liked the idea, Judge Leddy approved, and so, with these interesting twists, the trial began.

25

THE LONE
INTERROGATOR

If officials at Joe Arridy's trial had given a most-valuable-player award, as they do in sports, it would have gone to Cheyenne Sheriff George J. Carroll. Sheriff Carroll took the witness stand five different times. Judging from the number of transcript pages, he was up there much longer than any other witness.

After repeated cross-examinations, it slowly became clear that Carroll had interrogated Joe Arridy on Wednesday, August 26, for "six or seven hours" before District Attorney Taylor and detectives Horne and McDonald arrived in Cheyenne about 11 P.M. (p. 254). He testified that he was all alone when he interrogated Joe. Even after the three others arrived, he did all the late-night questioning in their presence. Chief of Police Grady claimed that the first of many calls between him and Sheriff Carroll occurred at 5:40 P.M. (p. 151).

And so, without notes or records of any kind, Sheriff Carroll told the court what he heard Joe say:

[Prosecutor Neary]: You stated you talked to Joe Arddy in Cheyenne first at the jail office.
[Sheriff Carroll]: Yes sir.
Q. You talked about various things and as to where he was from?
A. Yes sir.
Q. The second time you talked to him was how long after the first time?
A. Probably five or ten minutes.
Q. And there you talked to him in your office?
A. Yes.
Q. Who was present at that time, Sheriff?
A. Joe Arrdy and myself.
Q. No one else?
A. No one else.
Q. Will you state to the jury what you said to him at that time and what he answered, if you will, starting at the beginning and detailing it as you can remember it?
A. First, I started off by saying, "Well, Joe, you like the girls pretty well, don't you?"
    And he said Yes.
    I said, "You have had several girls during your lifetime."
    And he said Yes.
    I said, "If you like the girls so well, why did you hurt these two girls?"

He said, "I didn't mean to."

And I asked him how he hurt them. I didn't know what kind of instrument was used.

And he said, "With a club."

Well, that was satisfactory to me because I didn't know whether a club had been used or an axe, but in response to a question later on, some fifteen or twenty minutes later, he said he used a hatchet. I asked him what kind of hatchet it was.

He said it was a pretty good-sized hatchet, and indicated it.

I said, "Did it have a handle in it?"

He said Yes.

I said, "How long was it?"

He indicated again, very short handle, about that long (indicating).

And then I asked him if he knew these girls.

He said he didn't know their names.

I said, "Did you have a date with them?"

He said, "I met them on the street."

I said, "Where?"

He said, "In the park."

I said, "When?"

He said, "In the afternoon." And then he said that that night he went up to the house through the alley, over the back fence and into the yard.

Then I said, "What did you do when you got into the yard?"

He said he went into the bushes. And he said, "They were in the back yard."

I says, "How long did you stay there?"

He says, "Until the car went away."

I said, "Who got into a car?"

He said, "A man and a woman."

I said, "Then did you go into the house?"

He said, "No."

I said, "What did you do?"

He says, "I watched through the window."

I says, "What could you see?"

He said, "I could see some girls playing."

"Playing?"

"Playing."

I says, "What did you do then?"

He says, "I just stayed there."

"How long did you stay there?"

"Until the light went out."

"Then did you go into the house when the light went out?"

"No, we waited a little while."

"What for?"

"To let the girls go to sleep."

"How long did you wait?"

"Oh, ten or fifteen minutes."

"What did you do then?"

"We went into the house."

"How did you go in?"

"We went to the back door, but the back door was locked. Then I went around to the front door."

"Was the front door open?"

He said, "Yes. I went in the front door."

I says, "What did you do after you got in the front door?"

"I turned on the light"

"Where was the light?"

"To the left of the door. On this side of the door." He indicated with his left hand.

"What did you do then?"

"I went back in the next room."

"What room was that?"

He said, "Room where you sit down."

"What was the next room off of that?"

"Well," he said, "the bedroom."

I didn't know anything about the layout of the house, and that didn't sound right to me, but he said it was a bedroom. I said, "Did you go through the bedroom?"

He said, "No."

"Where did you go?"

"Went through kitchen. Then went back in the hall."

"Then where did you go?"

"In the room where the girls was."

"Was that room on your right or on your left?"

He said it was on the left.

"Was the door open?"

"Yes."

"When you got in there, what did you do?"

"Looked at the girls."

"Did you turn on the light?"

"Yes."

"How did it turn on?"

And he indicated, went over and reached up and turned it on.

"What did you see then?"

"Saw the girls."

"When you went in the door, was the girls' feet or their heads nearest to you?"

"Their feet."

"Which girl laid the nearest to you towards the door?"

He said, "The big one."

"Where was the little girl?"

"She was on the other side."

I asked him if there were any windows or doors in that room.

He said, "Yes there was three windows—two windows."

I said, "What could you see at the window?"

He said, "I could see bushes and the garden."

I said, "What was in the garden?"

"Flowers and bushes."

"What could you see out the other window?"

"A table."

That didn't sound right to me. I said, "Are you sure you saw a table out the window?"

He said Yes.

"What did you do then?"

"I hit them."

"Hit them?"

"I hit them."

I imagined he struck both of them. "What did you do then?"

"I took off my clothes."

"Did you take off all your clothes, Joe?"

"Yes."

"Where did you put them?"

"On the dresser."

"Where?"

"Right close to the bed." He indicated with his right hand.

"Did you take off your shoes?"

"Yes."

"Where did you put your shoes?"

"By the bed."

"What did you hit the girls with, a club?"

"No, I hit them with an axe." And that was when he described the axe.

"Then what did you do?"

"I got in bed with the girls."

"Did you have sexual intercourse?"

"I don't know what you mean."

I says, "What did you do to the girls?"

He says, "I screw 'em."

"Both of them?"

"No," he say, "not the little one. She is too little. I couldn't."

"What did you do then?"

"I got up, put on my clothes."

"Then what did you do?"

"I went out of the house."

"Did you go out the back door?"

"No, the back door was locked. I went out the front door."

"When you got out the front door, where did you go?"

"I went in the backyard."

"Did you go back out over the back fence?"

"No."

"Which way did you go?"

He says, "I go around the house and jump the fence" (pp. 82-86).

Carroll said that after leaving the house, Joe went to his mother's home. And according to Carroll, Joe had said that he was covered with blood, and his sister gave him a licking. Then Joe said, " They put me upstairs in the house. Made me hide."

Carroll then recalled that he left out one thing: "I asked him what he did with the hatchet. He said he hid it in his uncle's haystack. I asked him who his uncle was. He said his uncle's name was John Simony. I asked him where his uncle lived. He said in the steel works (pp. 87-88). But investigators never found a John Simony whom they could connect to the Arridy family or to the crime.

Carroll testified that on the evening of August 26, "I either called the chief or the chief called me, I believe, four or five times (p. 71).

Carroll also said that Chief Grady put Riley Drain on the phone. Drain asked questions which Carroll then asked Joe:

"What color was the bed?" Joe pointed to Carroll's golden oak table and said, "Just like this." The bed was tarnished brass.

"What color are the walls?" Joe pointed to Carroll's walls and said, "Just like this." Carroll reported that his walls were a "buff gray with a sort of yellowish tinge in it. The girls' walls were kalsomined yellow. Carroll continued:

Then [Drain] asked me to ask about different things in the room. I asked him and he answered. He said there was a door in the room, a dresser in the room, and a closet in the room, and he said there was some dresses hanging on the wall, that one was a red and one was a blue dress. I asked him the color of the nightgowns. He first said they were white, then then later on he said that one of them was a kind of pink. It was not pure white. I didn't know whether those answers were correct or not (p. 89).

Nor did the court ever learn whether these descriptions were correct.

Neary asked Carroll, "At the time Joe Arridy first admitted complicity, what were his reactions?"

"He was very sorry, he said, and cried about it."

"How many times did he cry after that?"

"I would say three or four times" (p. 93).

When Taylor, McDonald, and Horne arrived, Carroll said he continued to question Joe in front of the three men, "for the purpose of giving them what information I had gotten through this defendant." What was actually said during that late night session was never disclosed. Nor did Carroll or anyone else say how long this last session took. After it ended, however, there would be more sessions the next day, and the Cheyenne sheriff would relate most of the conversation to the court.

26

FRANK

On Wednesday, Joe Arridy had said nothing to Sheriff Carroll about an accomplice. But not so the next day. Carroll, Horne, McDonald, and Taylor were present when Pueblo District Attorney Taylor questioned Joe. Carroll told the court what took place:

> [Prosecutor Neary]: And can you state to the Court and jury what was the sum and substance of the conversation?
> [Sheriff Carroll]: The sum and substance of that conversation brought Frank Aguilar into the case.
> Q. How was that brought in, Sheriff?
> A. Next morning when we started questioning him, Mr. Taylor told him, "Joe, I want you to talk to us some more about this case," and says, "we want you to tell us the truth; are you willing to go ahead and tell us the truth?" Joe said he was. At that juncture Mr. Taylor turned to the detectives. I don't recall just which one, and asked for the axe that they had. After the hatchet was handed to him, he handed it to Joe. And asked Joe if he had ever seen that before. Joe says very pleasantly, kind of a grin on his face, Yes. He says, who does that hatchet belong to, Joe? He says, Frank.
> Q. Let me interrupt you; was the name Frank injected into this at any time prior to this by anyone?
> A. That is the first time I heard it mentioned (p. 91).

Carroll testified that Joe then described how he and Frank left the murder scene together, went to Frank's house, and washed the hatchet under a pump. "That is the way he put it, and they took it in and put it in a bucket under a lot of old rags, and that is the last he had seen of the hatchet" (p. 92). Shortly after that, the interrogations in Cheyenne ceased.

27

SECRET TRIP

How and when Joe Arridy got to Pueblo, and where he stayed, had been somewhat cloudy until Sheriff Carroll clarified the situation on the witness stand. This happened on Thursday afternoon after the morning when Joe allegedly had implicated Frank.

[Prosecutor Neary]: Did you bring him down to Pueblo?
[Sheriff Carroll]: Chief of Police Joe Cahill of Cheyenne, Wyoming, and myself. Yes.
Q. No one else in the car?
A. Except the defendant.
Q. Except the defendant. While you were bringing him down from Cheyenne. Will you state to the Court and Jury what were the actions of Joe Arddy?
A. Well the local authorities here were afraid of mob violence at that time, it appeared, and that was the reason it was arranged for us to bring him down. We changed our license plates to Colorado plates. And we told Joe he would have to remain hid in the car coming down, so we made him lay down in the back seat and remain out of sight en route down here to avoid any anticipated trouble, which he did; he stayed laying down in the seat all the way down.
Q. Did you tell him about the possibility of anticipated trouble?
A. No, we didn't discuss it with him (p. 92).

Carroll said that he and the chief took Joe to the Colorado State Hospital, where he was secretly housed that evening. Little Joe Arridy, the arrested vagrant, suddenly had become the center of a big case. And big cases called for big men. So the sheriff of Laramie County and the Cheyenne chief of police did the transporting themselves.

28

REENACTMENT

Sheriff Carroll told the court that he had stayed overnight after delivering Joe to the Colorado State Hospital. He described how he had helped Joe reenact the crime the next day.

> [Prosecutor Neary]: Will you explain to the Court and the jury who was with you when that was done?
>
> [Sheriff Carroll]: Detective Anderson, the defendant, Chief Cahill, and District Attorney Taylor. Well, I was driving the car, I believe it was that day. I think, as near as I remember. I was driving the car, and we drove over [to the Drain residence] after precautions had been made by the police to fully protect anything that might develop. We drove to a point near an alley, some block or block and a half from the house. Detective Anderson and I drove on around the block and met [Taylor, Cahill, and Joe] out near the front door. Then we went in and reenacted the crime in the house.
>
> Q. All right, state what he did, Sheriff?
>
> A. Just as we come in the door, I asked him where he turned on the light. He reached over and up under a shade, lamp shade, and turned on a floor lamp light. Then we asked him to go over the same route that he did the night of the murder to the bedroom. He went directly through the parlor, through the kitchen into the hall, and to the left into the bedroom where the murder had occurred. When we got in there, I asked him to show me how he turned the light on in there. He walked over and reached up and turned on a globe light that hung from the ceiling. Then I asked him different things he had told me about in the room, and got him to point them out to me again, which he did readily (pp. 95-96).

Carroll explained in great detail that the backyard was exactly as Joe had described it during the interrogation in Cheyenne—the bushes, the flowers, the bench under one of the windows.

Carroll then drove Joe back to the office of Pueblo Police Chief Grady. Things did not look good for Joe.

Interestingly, only Sheriff Carroll testified about the reenactment. District Attorney French Taylor was no longer on the case. All the detectives named in the newspaper as attending were absent. And Detective Anderson did not testify about it. Neither did the Cheyenne chief of police. Only the Cheyenne sheriff described what happened.

29

CONFRONTATION

After Carroll told the court about driving Joe to Chief Grady's office, he described what happened:

> [Carroll]: After that, he was brought back there and held in the Chief's office while Aguilar was brought in. There had been nothing said previous to that, with reference to the case, but when Aguilar was brought into the office, Mr. Taylor asked [Joe] who that was. He said, "That's Frank." Frank spoke up and said, "I never seen him before" (p. 95).

Later, Chief Grady testified that the confrontation took place in front of himself, "Sheriff Carroll, Chief of Police Joe Cahill from Cheyenne, Everett Horne, Richard Anderson, French Taylor, and other officers" (p. 150).

30

TO CANON CITY

After Carroll described the face-off between Joe and Frank, there was one more leg in the journey that had to be mentioned.

[Prosecutor Neary]: That was all that was done at that time?
[Carroll]: Yes, except to deliver them on to the penitentiary later that day.
Q. Delivered them both to the penitentiary?
A. Yes sir.

Although he didn't mention it, the entourage that delivered Joe and Frank to the penitentiary was elaborate. There were two Colorado State Patrol cruisers: The first car contained the two defendants, along with four law-enforcement officers; the second car was filled with six more officers. Carroll and Cahill followed in their car, now bearing their original Wyoming plates.

The legendary chaser of the Barker gang and the Boettcher kidnappers, and now the apprehender of famous Joe Arridy, enjoyed a reunion with Warden Roy Best. Then, the job finished, Carroll and Cahill headed for Cheyenne.

On the stand, Carroll must have been a powerful presence. His testimony must have impressed the jury, partly because he sounded so veteran, so weathered, so sure. A tough, detail-by-detail criminal lawyer might have flustered him during cross-examination.

But that didn't happen with Barnard. He was too busy trying to prove that Joe was insane. So when, in his cross, he might have come close to some pay-dirt questions, he broke off with other questions, such as, "When did you first discover Joe Arrdy was an imbecile?" or "Is it not true that you once said, 'Joe Arrdy is a nut'?"

Toward the end of one cross-examination, Barnard did ask some interesting questions:

[Defender Barnard]: You seem to remember, Mr. Carroll, the details of this case as related to you by Joe Arddy, very clearly, don't you?
[Carroll]: Rather clearly, the important phases of it.
Q. You have gone over the facts in this case time and again, both with police officers and with Mr. Neary—or Mr. Taylor?
Q. To some extent, yes.
Q. And that is what fixed it firmly in your mind?
A. That is largely why I have a clear picture of it (p. 125-26).

With Carroll as the prime evidence giver, others took the stand and reinforced his testimony with times and locations, for the most part. But none of it altered Carroll's version of the confession. So when I came to this point in the transcript, I wanted to say, "Go get him, defender."

But Barnard responded, "No further questions."

31

THE GIBSONS

Sheriff Carroll finally ended the elaborate story about obtaining the confession and his travels back and forth along the eastern slope of the Colorado Rockies. After he stepped down, the next two witnesses presented the court with an interesting interlude. Mr. and Mrs. Glen Gibson had been subpoenaed to identify a shirt with a tear in the left shoulder—the one purportedly ripped by Irene O'Driscoll in Colorado Springs; the one with blood on the inside; the one-time white institutional shirt belonging to Grand Junction inmate Peter Clauson; the one now turned to a greasy and grimy gray. The Gibsons identified the shirt, and then they probably offered more than the prosecution expected (pp. 126-46).

The Gibsons ran a kitchen car for a Union Pacific "extra gang." On August 20, they were setting up their work camp in the East Cheyenne railroad yards. At about 2:30 P.M., a scruffy Joe Arridy came up to the car and offered to work for food. They had a busy crew, and Mrs. Gibson put Joe to work washing dishes right away.

Since it was a depression year, everyone was used to having people come to their door to work for food. Then they usually left. But Joe stayed on.

When it became clear that he wanted to stay, Mrs. Gibson focused on his shirt. "I asked him if the police officers had caught him in the railroad yards and beat him up." Joe said nothing.

"What's your name?" Joe said nothing again.

"What shall I call you?" "Joe."

Later, he tried to give them his last name. "He said Arddy—Hardy; we thought he spelled it H-A-R-D-Y. His language was broken, and we didn't understand" (p. 132).

Mrs. Gibson told him to take off the shirt, and she gave him some clean underwear and a clean khaki shirt from her husband's supply. Joe placed the torn shirt out by a washtub containing dirty dish towels. Later, when Mrs. Gibson washed the towels, she thought about washing the shirt, too, but it was too dirty. She left it alongside the tracks.

Joe stayed with the Gibsons even when the crew moved on to Archer, nine miles east of Cheyenne. Then the extra gang prepared to move much farther east, and since Joe wasn't an authorized employee, he had to leave the crew. On the afternoon of August 26, Mrs. Gibson drove Joe back to Cheyenne—back to the railroad yards. Later that day, he was arrested by the two railroad detectives.

On August 30, a sheriff came to talk to the Gibsons about Joe Arridy. Later that day, Mrs. Gibson took the officer to where she had left the torn shirt beside the railroad tracks.

There was little doubt, from the Gibsons' testimony, that they liked Joe. Of course, they probably had been "prepped" to do little more than identify the shirt. Mrs. Gibson made it plain that all of the time he was in the camp, she and Joe worked side by side. "He helped me," she said, "He and I together." During cross-examination, she was drawn out some more:

[Defender Barnard]: The other things you talked to him about, Mrs. Gibson, did he answer you readily?

[Mrs. Gibson]: We didn't talk very much. We were all awfully busy; Joe worked hard, and we did, too.

Q. He never opened up a conversation with you or any one else in your presence?

A. Not at that time.

Q. Did he at any time?

A. Several times in the evening, while we were eating, he may have said something.

Q. I mean, did he open the conversation?

A. No sir. Oh, he asked about different things.

Q. What did he say?

A. For instance, if there was anything to be done, he asked us if he should do this or do that to help us. And we would say yes; and there wasn't a day went by that he didn't ask me if he wasn't going to leave that day, because most always if you feed anybody, they are getting ready to leave your camp right away.

Q. But he did not talk very much.

A. We didn't have time to talk, but he answered questions and asked questions.

Q. He did things you told him to without any objection, didn't he?

A. He sure did.

Q. Went ahead and did it?

A. Did it very well.

Q. You showed him how to do it?

A. Never showed him how to do anything.

Q. You did the planning?

A. Yes sir.

Q. Was he a good worker?

A. Very good, the best helper I ever had on the outfit, as far as being clean and never complaining about anything he did (pp. 132-33).

Mrs. Gibson's testimony led to a clearer view of the ripped-up shirt. When its discovery was heralded in the region's newspapers on August 31, the officers announced their plan to do all kinds of tests on the blood stains. Then when Defender Barnard cross-examined Mrs. Gibson, arguments ensued over whether the stains were human blood or animal blood, or possibly not blood at all. It then became clear that the prosecution had failed to do any testing on the shirt at all. This left the jury to guess for themselves what the stains might have been (pp. 135-37).

The Gibsons obviously saved Joe from his confession that he had assaulted Irene O'Driscoll in Colorado Springs on August 23 (White, 1936b). They also saved him from Miss O'Driscoll's identification, and her statement that he without a doubt was her attacker and that she probably ripped his shirt. When Colorado Springs Chief Harper and Miss O'Driscoll traveled to Canon City to confirm the charge, he told the press that "no positive identification" had been made.

32

MISSING CONFESSION

The confession that Frank Aguilar signed with an "X" was never presented as evidence in Joe Arridy's case. What happened to that confession in Joe Arridy's trial can be explained quickly. Detective Everett Horne was on the witness stand.

[Prosecutor Neary]: Were you at the Canon City penitentiary at Canon City, Colorado, on September 2, 1936?

[Mr. Horne]: I was.

Q. I hand you Plaintiff's Exhibit P [The confession signed by Aguilar], and without stating its contents, Officer Horne, will you state to the Court and jury what that is?

A. This is the statement of the happening, what took place at the Drain home August 15, 1936.

Q. Who made the statement?

A. Frank Aguilar made the statement.

Q. Was there anyone present when that statement was made?

A. There was.

Q. Who was present?

A. There was the warden of the penitentiary, Roy Best; a guard by the name of Roy Montgomery, Art Wilson, Officer McDonald, French Taylor, myself, and Joe Arrdy.

Q. I will ask you to examine the last page of that exhibit and state, if you can and will, what signatures appear thereon, and if you were present when these signatures were placed on that instrument?

A. I was present when those signatures were placed here, signed by Frank Aguilar with his mark, witnessed by Roy Montgomery, Joe Arrdy [an interesting placement of Joe's name, since his was on the bottom margin], J. Leo Sterling, Roy Best, W. L. McDonald, and myself.

[MR. NEARY]: We offer in evidence, if Your Honor please, People's Exhibit P.

[MR. BARNARD]: I will object to the introduction of this (pp. 156-59).

Then, with no hassle before Judge Leddy regarding the admissible nature of the document, Mr. Neary merely said, "We will withdraw it."

The words of that confession never found their way into the trial documents of *People v Joe Arrdy*. It appears in chapter 19 only because *The Chieftain* printed it in its entirety on September 3, 1936.

33

ONE SINGLE HAIR

Part of the jury's job was to view exhibits and think about them. They looked at photos of the bloody bed and the wounds on the Drain girls' heads. They saw two bloody pillows and the bed clothing that was taken out of a cardboard box and unrolled for them. There was that hatchet—the one that was purported to fit neatly into the gashes of both girls' heads. Then, of course, there was that filthy, ripped shirt. To a thinking member of the jury, these items would not seem to connect Joe strongly to the crime scene.

But another exhibit did. It connected Joe, even though the jury didn't have a chance to see it. Dr. Frances McConnell took the stand with a microscope slide of two hairs which she claimed were identical. This was the same toxicologist who testified at Frank Aguilar's trial, the one who worked at all Denver hospitals, primarily doing lab work on hay-fever allergies and the common cold. There were no forensic criminalists in 1937 as there are today, but Dr. McConnell, without a doubt, was brilliant, well-focused, and totally objective in whatever laboratory work she undertook.

She stated under oath that she had received a sealed envelope, labeled "Hairs taken from bed sheets and pillows from the Drain home, 1536 Stone." She said it was "delivered to me in my office, 510 Republic Building, Denver, the 26th of August by detectives McDonald and Horne." She said she thought that her appointment with them had been at 4:00 P.M. (p. 52).

She said the envelope contained "a mass of hairs; a few fibers, and they were matted together with blood." She separated the mass by soaking it in distilled water. In the mass, she found a single darkly pigmented hair. It was two and a quarter inches long. It was "soaked in alcohol quite a length of time, and then in zylol, to bring out its characteristics and cellular structure." She said that she made cross sections "which would help one to make a study of the medullar characteristics and also of the orbit."

At the time, she had found nothing to match the hair. Then on August 31, she received, via registered mail, a box containing two envelopes from Detective McDonald. The envelopes were labeled "Hair from the chest of Joe Arddy" and "Hair from the head of Joe Arddy." They were hairs taken from Joe Arridy in Sheriff Carroll's office on the morning of August 27. After putting them through the same process as before and comparing them, she concluded that the earlier hair and Joe's hair were identical. To prove it, she set up a microscope, and Prosecutor Neary invited the jurors to come down, one by one, look into the microscope at the two hairs, and see for themselves.

Defender Barnard stopped the process with an objection: "Dr. McConnell has testified that she is an expert, and it takes an expert to tell the difference or similarity between such things as hairs. I can't see how it possibly would help the jury to have a look at these hairs through this microscope, because they are laymen, the same as I am" (p. 55).

With that, Prosecutor Neary withdrew the offer and the jurors remained in their box.

During cross-examination, Dr. McConnell made it clear that she did not know to whom the hairs belonged. She made the claim that "among people whose hair appears grossly the same, about two in five hundred will be identical, probably." When Barnard asked if she knew the race of the person from whom the hair came, Dr. McConnell stated that the race of the person would be related to "the American Indian" (p. 58).

Later, through cross-examination, it was learned that the bedding was rolled up and put in a box shortly after the crime. The box was stored in a busy office in the Pueblo Police Department, and the matted sample was taken from the bedding on the morning of August 26 and delivered to Denver in the afternoon.

Barnard, of course, raised serious questions as to why this evidence, picked up on August 16, was not delivered until August 26. No plausible explanations were ever recorded—just the specific times and actions. But Dr. McConnell made it clear that the sample with the single dark hair was in her hands at about the same time Joe Arridy began his first confession to Sheriff Carroll.

34

THE PAWNBROKER

The last witness for the prosecution was Saul Kahn, a pawnbroker at Kahn's Loan Company at 219 South Union, some twenty blocks northwest of the crime scene. He claimed that Joe came into his store "on August 15 at about four or five o'clock in the afternoon." He bought a gun.

Defender Barnard opened his cross-examination by asking Kahn to estimate the number of people who come to his store: "Sometimes fifty, sometimes twenty-five. It all depends."

[Barnard]: Been a lot of people in here, haven't there?
[Kahn]: Yes sir.
Q. You come in here and say you know the defendant was in there on that day, how do you know?
A. Because it happened a policeman came in and he happened to notice the name of Joe Arddy on our gun book.
Q. Where is this book now?
A. He has got it over there.
Q. You wrote it down?
A. Yes.
Q. That is how you remember that this happened?
A. When a man comes in and buys a gun, we pay no attention, but when a man comes in that isn't bright, we notice him.
Q. You say a bright fellow?
A. Oh the fellow come in and talked quite a while.
Q. What would you consider him?
A. I consider he wasn't bright.

The name Kahn wrote down in the book was "Joseph Arrdy." During redirect examination, Kahn added more details:

[Assistant Prosecutor Keen]: Have you seen Joseph Arddy since that date, the man who purchased the gun?
[Kahn]: No, the only time I seen him was up at the city jail.
Q. When was that?
A. Five or six days after he bought the gun.

Q. What were the circumstances?
A. Well, they called me over to the city jail to identify him. When I got over, the minute I looked at him he was the man who bought the gun.

RE-CROSS-EXAMINATION

[Defender Barnard]:
Q. Did they take you down and point out Joe Arddy to you?
A. There is Joe Arddy [pointing].
Q. You didn't get my question. Did anybody point out Joe to you at the station?
A. I should say not.
Q. You picked him out yourself.
A. I picked him out myself.

❑ ❑ ❑

If Joe purchased the gun downtown on August 15 at "four or five o'clock in the afternoon," this means that he walked the twenty blocks to Bessemer before he met Frank Aguilar.

35

BARNARD'S DEFENSE

After Saul Kahn stepped down and Prosecutor Neary rested his case, Defender Barnard rose to his feet. Now was the time to put his defense witnesses on the stand. But before he did, he delivered his own opening argument that the court allowed him to postpone until this moment:

Gentlemen of the Jury:

Now comes my turn to tell you gentlemen what the evidence of the defendant, Joe Arddy, will be, with reference to this horrible crime, we have seen brought forth. . . . The testimony of the defendant will show that the defendant does not know, nor do I know, nor do any of these officers that have testified know, whether Joe Arrdy was there or not.

Our testimony will show that this young man was incompetent, was so insane as not to know what he was doing; so insane as not to know what he was saying to the officers; that he could be led into saying anything people wanted him to say or admitting any crime he is charged with, and it will further show that when this purported confession or statement was taken from him by these officers, that he he didn't know what he was doing or what he was saying. And the testimony will further show that he didn't know anything; his mind is so weak, he is so insane that there is no question about voluntariness or involuntariness of the statement which George Carroll testified to.

The evidence has already shown, of course, that the defendant, Joe Arddy, has told two or three different stories about what happened, and it will further show that he will tell these stories and tell it differently about each one. He doesn't know what is going on in Court today; he doesn't know what this is all about. It will show that he is an imbecile, that he is a child between the ages of four and six. . . .

The testimony will further show that it is impossible for this boy to tell the difference between right and wrong or the difference between good and evil, to such an extent that he may be led or he may be sent to do anything under the sun, and he will do it; that he will be led to say anything under the sun you ask him, and gentlemen, in saying that I don't know and the States' witnesses don't know; this Court doesn't know whether or not this boy was there or what part he played in this thing, if any; I can't know; no one knows. . . .

And at the close of the evidence, gentlemen, we will ask you to return a verdict of not guilty by reason of insanity at the time of the perpetration of the crime charged, and since (pp. 162-65).

36

DOCTORTALK II

The Colorado State Hospital psychiatrists were back for the defense. This time they brought an extra "heavy" in Dr. Benjamin L. Jefferson, the superintendent of the institution at Grand Junction. This time they planned to get it right. They would all say again that Joe Arridy was an imbecile with the mentality of a child not older than six and a half years. They would drive home repeatedly their litany of the placement of persons with feeblemindedness—idiots (zero to three years), imbeciles (three to eleven years) and morons (eleven to twelve years), although some of them varied on the age groupings. They would say that clinically, Joe was not insane. But in a legal sense, he was very insane.

They would reiterate that Joe often had admitted to wrongs that other people did. They would say again that he hardly ever spoke unless he was coaxed by questions. He usually spoke three-word sentences. He was "phlegmatic" and "droll," which explained why he sat so quietly in the courtroom, barely moving, staring straight ahead, like an Indian brave freshly captured by the U.S. Calvary.

Then with all the forcefulness they could muster, they would say one more time that Joe Arridy could not tell right from wrong or good from evil, *with respect to the crime.* During the sanity trial, Prosecutor Neary talked them all over the lot about when Joe knew the difference and when he didn't. This time they had to be ready.

Superintendent Jefferson led off. He shared his first-hand observations of Joe at the institution.

His Work in the Kitchen:

Joe has never been a boy that mingled with the other boys very much. He limited himself to two or three boys. I put him in the charge of Mrs. Bowers in the dining room. His mental age would only permit him to do certain things; scrubbing, washing dishes, carrying in coal and water; not very reliable in doing errands . . . he had broken his key in the door to the meat closet, bringing up sausage or something else when she sent him for pears or peaches (pp. 171-72).

On Taking Blame:

In the case about cigarettes; he took some cigarettes, some packages; he acknowledged that he took these things, when we know he didn't, that some of the other boys took them (p. 174).

On His Perversions:

Both as to masturbation and with boys? Well, yes, they sometimes—not entirely masturbating. We have segregated them and it isn't done . . . we separated them. They were all thrown in dormitories there, and after I went there I took the perverse fellows and put a good one with him. Now his partner doesn't do anything at all (p. 189).

On His Attraction to Women:

Mrs. Bowers in her kitchen and dining room, she has about ten boys and about eight to ten girls. In view of his perverse habits, we watched him as to whether he ever peeped or looked at any girls. And he never did (p. 171). . . .

[Barnard]: Have you ever known him to care anything about women?
A. No sir.
Q. Has he ever given any indication that he cared anything about them?
A. Not in the six years I have been there (p. 199).

Superintendent Jefferson asked to read his prepared statement about why Joe was the way he was:

In the makeup of this boy, which comes into the question of whether he understands right from wrong and good from evil, I must go back, taking in his family history; taking in his everyday actions and my classification of this boy from study over years past, and tell you the reason that I will answer "Yes" and "No" on this question.

We have a child here that was sent to the state institution several years before I went there, and I have gone into the history of his parents, and Joe's history.

I have classified him as a primary ament, hereditary. I took his heredity record and worked up from there to the point of view of his primary birth. He was brought into the world as he is today from a diseased plasma, an ament. . . .

That is, a diseased germ plasma that never was allowed to unfold, but has inflicted upon this boy abundant damage all of his life. This condition, through habit and all, has followed him through environment on up. He has reverted to perverse conditions which were bad. These things have all been gone into and that is the reason for my placement of him, as I did, a high-low imbecile, hereditary. . . .

He does not have it as a high moron, who is absolutely a moral deviate, and is absolutely responsible for his acts in a higher degree than they are (pp. 179-81).

As he read his statement, one could get the feeling that Henry H. Goddard was riding again. The only problem was that Jefferson was on the stand in an attempt to save a life. In 1937, Goddard's diseased-germ-plasma talk was moving Adolph Hitler to stop such stuff from spreading by killing anybody who had it. And in 1937, many upstanding citizens of our country admired Germany in its struggle for a pure-blooded Nordic race.

Dr. Jefferson stated that he also had written out his investigation of Joe and the boys who ran away and hitched rides on the freight cars. He was asked not to read that one.

Dr. J. L. Rosenblum, Dr. F. H. Zimmerman, and Paul S. Wolf all took the stand, and Defender Barnard enabled each to reel off the same psychosocial litany, but in a briefer fashion. Then when Prosecutor Neary cross-examined them, one by one, he allowed them to go on and on about some of their pet psychological statements. Rosenblum expounded on what the term *phlegmatic* meant ("Apathetic . . . of a temperament which is not boisterous; not given to overactivity, not given to sudden changes of emotions.") He was asked, "What is the opposite?" ("I don't like to tell you, erethic . . . characteristically by smiling, very active, purposeless movements—things of that sort"). Neary led Rosenblum to say, at different times, that Joe was a nervous person and that he wasn't a nervous person. At times the spectators laughed.

Then Neary said to Rosenblum, "Supposing I asked you, 'Do you know Dorothy Drain?' Is there anything in that question that suggests the answer?"

Rosenblum responded, "I don't think the way Joe does, so I couldn't tell whether it was suggestive or not." (The audience broke into laughter, and Judge Leddy said to the spectators that if it happened again, he would clear the court.) Later, Neary led Rosenblum to say that he knew everything about Joe's mind.

Neary and Wolf got into a fencing match over the fact that Joe told the doctor that his fountain pen was an *ink pencil*. Neary thought that was more accurate than a *fountain pen*, since there was no fountain in it. That led to *automobile* verses *gas carriage*, the *blindfolded lady* versus *justice*, and *pencil* versus *lead pencil*, since there was no lead in it. And so it went, Dr. Abstract clashing with Mr. Concrete—with the jury obviously siding with the latter. Neary was moving those doctors around the ring like a lion tamer. Then he cracked the whip and hit them with a litany of his own:

> Assuming a man had committed the crime of rape and murder, left the town in which the murder was committed; he couldn't read or write; he was at a camp, engaged in work for six days during that time, traveling on freight trains and stopping at other junctions, and he were picked up and gave complete information as to the major features, details of the crime which had been committed, would you say that that man was an imbecile? (p. 236).

Here was the scene: The doctors did their best to stretch the truth one way, and the prosecutor did his best to pull it as far as he could the other way. And yet Joe Arridy just sat there, staring forward. The jury soon would have to decide whether Joe's mind was a blank or whether he knew everything that was going on in the room.

❑ ❑ ❑

After the defense rested, things speeded up. Neary called his rebuttal witnesses to the stand, and each delivered a short, well-aimed statement:

Detective Everett Horne, a police officer with fifteen years experience with many different types of men: Neary asked, "Based upon that experience and your observation of Joe Arddy, you may state in your opinion, whether or not Joe Arddy has the capacity to distinguish between right and wrong, good and evil." Horne answered, "In my opinion he has."

Hugh D. Harper, Chief of Police, Colorado Springs, an officer since 1903, who had visited Joe at Canon City for an hour and a half—regarding whether Joe had assaulted Irene

O'Driscoll: "Based on your experience, [does] Joe Arrdy have the mental power to accept the good and refrain from evil?" Harper answered, "He has."

George J. Carroll, Sheriff of Laramie County, Wyoming, with thirty years experience, who had interrogated Joe for "six or seven hours": "Based on your experience [is] Joe Arridy capable of distinguishing between right and wrong?" Carroll answered, "I think there is no doubt, whatever, but what he is."

The rebuttals came across like howitzer shots, and within a few hours, the jury received the case (pp. 249-56).

❏ ❏ ❏

After three hours and 25 minutes, and four ballots, the jury rendered its verdict:

We, the Jury, find the defendant Joe Arddy guilty of murder in the first degree, in manner and form as charged in the information, and fix his penalty at death.

Joe's response was recorded in *The Pueblo Chieftain:*

SUNDAY, APRIL 18, 1937, EDITION

Arridy received the verdict unflinchingly as he sat in the courtroom under the watchful eye of Rudolph Martin, warden at the county jail, where Arridy has been quartered during the trial. Seemingly he took no notice of the pronouncement of the death verdict as delivered by Jury Foreman Charles H. Beecher.

Only his eyes shifted uneasily and became somewhat red. They were still red several minutes later as Sheriff Lewis Worker led him away to the car that sped him to the death house at Canon City penitentiary, although he was able to grin sheepishly at deputy sheriffs who spoke to him in the hallway.

REJECTION

On June 25, 1937, Joe Arridy was placed in front of Judge Harry Leddy. The judge spoke:

> And thereupon the said defendant, Joe Arddy, is brought to the bar of this Court and it is inquired of him if anything he has to say why judgment of the law should not now be pronounced against him upon the verdict of the Jury heretofore rendered in this cause, and he answers nothing.
>
> Thereupon it is ordered, adjudged and considered by the Court that it is the grave and solemn sentence of this Court under and by virtue of the verdict of the Jury rendered herein, that you, Joe Arddy, shall be remanded to the custody of the Sheriff of this County and State; that within three days from this date you shall be taken by the said Sheriff and delivered into the custody of the Warden of the penitentiary of this State at Canon City, that you shall be by the said Warden of said penitentiary kept in solitary confinement until the week beginning October 10th and ending October 16th next, and upon a day and hour in said week to be designated by said Warden you shall be taken from said place of confinement to the place of execution within the confines of said penitentiary, and then and there shall be inflicted upon you the punishment of death by the administration of lethal gas as by statute provided.

The People of the State of Colorado versus Joe Arrdy
Case Number 24733
In the Pueblo District Court, Pueblo County, Colorado.

FISHING FOR CONGRATULATIONS

In Governor Edward C. Johnson's papers, now housed in the Colorado State Archives in Denver, I found the following telegram:

CHEYENNE WYO 7:10 PM SEPT 9 36
GOV. EDWARD C. JOHNSON
DENVER
SINCERE CONGRATULATIONS YOU SURE GOT THE JOB DONE
T.J. CAHILL
GEORGE J. CARROLL

I also found the following letter:

September 10, 1936
Mr. George Carroll
Sheriff
Cheyenne
Wyoming

Dear Mr. Carroll:

All of Colorado appreciated the splendid job you did in solving the Drain murder case at Pueblo. It is just such alertness on the part of police officers that make it impossible for the criminal to escape.

If I were to suggest something to the underworld, I would advise them to detour around Cheyenne because of Sheriff George J. Carroll and Chief T. J. Cahill.

Colorado congratulates you for your efficiency in office.

Sincerely,

Ed C. Johnson
Governor

39

REWARD

Like the last baseball game in the World Series, some people celebrate, while others hurt. Such was the case when an August 11, 1937, *Chieftain* headline announced:

THREE MEN TO RECEIVE $1,000 CHECK ON SAME DAY
FRANK AGUILAR DIES FOR SEX SLAYING OF GIRL

A $1,000 reward had been posted by the city and county governments for information leading to the arrest and conviction of the party or parties who murdered Dorothy Drain. The three celebrated recipients were Sheriff George J. Carroll of Cheyenne, Wyoming, as well as George R. Burnett and Carl M. Christenson, Union Pacific Railroad special agents at Cheyenne.

A Colorado and Wyoming sheriffs' association convention was scheduled to be held in Pueblo on Friday, August 13, the same day Frank Aguilar was to be executed. At the convention, a special proclamation was read:

Whereas Joe Arridy was arrested near Cheyenne, Wyo. by George R. Burnett and Carl M. Christenson, special officers, and George J. Carroll, sheriff of Laramie county, Wyo. and

Whereas the subsequent confession obtained by said officers from Joe Arridy resulted in his conviction of Frank Aguilar for said crime, now therefore be it resolved by the Council of Pueblo

That since George J. Carroll, George R. Burnett, and Carl M. Christenson, by their action in said arrest and subsequent confession fully met the terms of the offer of said reward, are entitled to the same.

Therefore, be it further resolved that the sum of $500 so offered be paid to George J. Carroll, George R. Burnett, and Carl M. Christenson from the legal and contingent fund and to no other persons, in full settlement and satisfaction of said reward offered by the city.

❏ ❏ ❏

Being depression times, when one could buy a pound of ground round for a dime, and a quart of milk with a topping of rich cream for a nickel, $500 was big money—it could even buy a new car!

GOOD-BYE, FRANK

Frank Aguilar chewed gum as he stood before the judge for sentencing. Judge William B. Stewart asked Aguilar whether he had anything to say before the death sentence was imposed. Aguilar stood quietly for some time, his jaws working rapidly on the gum. Then he scratched his head and said, "I don't know what to say." The only emotion he showed was a slowing of the movement of his jaws as the death sentence was being read (TPC, 2-4-37).

Aguilar's final death date was Friday, August 13, just two days short of the anniversary of Dorothy Drain's murder. On Thursday morning, he shed tears in a meeting with Warden Roy Best.

"My tears are not for myself," he said. "They are for the mamma, and for my wife and three babies." Later he said, "I know I am going to die Friday night. I will be prepared. I will go bravely, with a smile on my lips." Then he became calm and impassive.

Aguilar's last day followed a well-planned ritual. One might even have likened it to an act of worship in a religious congregation—one in which a sequence of well-orchestrated steps slowly but surely pulls everyone toward a common focus—an ultimate climax. The penitentiary needed such an "order of service," outlining who does what and when, right down to the strapping of arms and legs to a chair at 8:05 P.M.

At the beginning of the day, Father Albert Schaller, the prison chaplain, received Aguilar's confession, then gave him Holy Communion.

His aged mother, his wife, and three children came to visit. As they were leaving, Aguilar's mother collapsed in front of his cell. As she lay unconscious on the death-house floor, Aguilar ignored her and continued talking to guards.

The next three hours were spent in his cell with Father Schaller. A table was set in the corridor outside his cell for his last meal, which he and the chaplain ate together. It was a simple meal, in accordance with Roman Catholic tradition—tomato soup, fried eggs, toast, french-fried potatoes, coffee, and donuts. Guard Roy Montgomery and Warden Roy Best looked on.

After the meal, Aguilar and Father Schaller sat together in the cell, speaking to each other in Spanish until Warden Best appeared with the death warrant. Aguilar stood in front of his cell door, his arms folded, and listened as Warden Best read the warrant, as required by law. When Best asked Aguilar if he understood, he grinned, unfolded his arms, and shook the warden's hand.

Then began the procession to the top of Woodpecker Hill, the highest hill on the grounds of the penitentiary. Aguilar exited death row with the warden on his left and the chaplain on his right. Once outside, a crowd of witnesses and media people joined the procession as it headed up the long hill. Everyone walked quietly, listening as the three leaders spoke to one another. Aguilar puffed on a cigar, arms folded in front of him.

Since the road to the top could be seen through many windows in the scattered buildings, other inmates watched the procession in silence.

At the top of the hill they came upon a small one-room cottage, with a peaked roof and two large bay windows in the front. The witnesses and reporters stood outside the bay windows and looked in. Front and center was Riley Drain, the father of Dorothy Drain.

Aguilar entered the cottage through a back door and shortly reappeared in the windows wearing only his shorts.

He entered a large, egg-shaped steel chamber, sat down in the center of three seats, and the guards began their well-practiced movements, strapping his arms, legs, and body to the chair. Then the guards said their good-byes, each reaching down and clasping his bound hand. Father Schaller gave him the church's blessing, and Aguilar pressed his lips to the priest's hand. Guard Roy Montgomery, who had witnessed his "X" on his confession, gently tugged at a lock of Aguilar's hair.

Then the acid vats, which had been prepared by the prison physician, were moved into place on each side of the chair. The cyanide eggs were positioned above the vats. A heavy steel door was slammed shut, locked, and made air tight. A signal was given by Warden Best, and in a matter of minutes, Frank Aguilar was gone.

Where Aguilar went may be a matter of conjecture. But where he intended to go, and what he intended to do, was made plain during his walk to the top of Woodpecker Hill. His spoken intentions were published in newspapers throughout the region.

Earlier, he had made a pact with soon-to-die Willis Wynn in the next cell: "Wynn and I are going to farm in heaven," he said. "We'll raise black-seed watermelons and sheep and hogs and corn and vegetables—yes, and cotton, so that we can hire niggers to pick it" (Osborne, 1937).

41

ONE-OF-A-KIND WARDEN

If Roy Phelix Best applied for a job as warden of a state penitentiary today, he wouldn't have a ghost of a chance. The hiring commission would simply say that he just didn't have the right stuff—no proper training, no psychological education, no management experience. Furthermore, he didn't even *look* like an executive. Here was this big bear of a guy with a pudgy face, the sad dark eyes of a bassett hound, and a delightful mischievous grin. He wore suits that all too quickly seemed to fall into disarray on his barrel-chested frame. A Mafia boss maybe, but not a prison warden.

And yet, picture a man who grew up on a homestead cattle ranch outside of Rocky Ford, Colorado. He became a top bronc rider and steer wrestler who followed the rodeo circuit, even performing in Madison Square Garden. Picture the man leaving the rodeo life to become a patrolman for the Colorado Courtesy Patrol, now known as the State Patrol. Picture him on October 3, 1929, after two years of service as a patrolman, being dispatched to the Colorado State Penitentiary to help quell a riot started by five crazed inmates who tried to shoot their way to freedom. By the next day, eight guards had been shot and thrown into the yard from upper-story windows, and the inner prison buildings were gutted by fire, machine-gun bullets, and dynamite. The riot ended when the ringleader turned his gun on his pals and then upon himself.

What followed was chaos. Twelve hundred inmates were housed in tents while work crews began to rebuild the prison. After a year, the prisoners had only increased their sullen behavior, and another riot took place in February 1930. Finally, Governor William H. "Billy" Adams decided to clean house. The warden was fired, and a search began for one who could manage the problem. Patrolman Best had been the governor's driver for a time, and he was sent to Canon City as acting warden for thirty days. Those thirty-day stints were renewed several times, until Governor Adams appointed Best deputy warden in January 1931. A year and a half later, at age thirty-one, he was made the warden.

What Best did at the prison has become the stuff of legends. He developed imperatives that everyone was expected to live by: "Discipline without tyranny"; "Prisoners are human beings"; with the added proviso that they are to be treated as such, as long as they act like human beings; "Lots of work and lots of play; no work, no play." With this imperative, the inmates rebuilt the prison themselves:

Surmounting almost unbelievable difficulties, Warden Best has literally made a mountain come to him! Through shrewd planning and the use of materials at hand, he has utilized prison labor to convert the huge limestone and granite mountain at the rear of the prison grounds into model concrete cell houses and industrial buildings. His building accomplishments are little less than miraculous, when the cost in actual dollars and cents is considered. For instance, neither the $400,000 new cell house Number 7, nor the $350,000 dining hall cost the taxpayers of Colorado a penny for labor. The steel for the framework came "knocked down" from the mills, and the prisoners poured every ounce of concrete, put in every screw and bolt, and even installed the entire heating plant.

Best has made it possible for every one of the more than a thousand inmates to be housed in a clean, fireproof, comfortable, sanitary, *separate* cell. Each man after the day's work is done, can if he chooses, follow a hobby, listen to a radio program, enjoy a bowl of roses or peonies on his table or his own canary or simply rest undisturbed (Spring, 1945).

Best insisted on the privacy of single cells to put an end to "abominable behavior"—especially predatory attacks. He also insisted on periods when talking was not allowed between cells. He felt that the inmates needed such times of utter privacy. But he despised solitary confinement and replaced it with any alternative he could dream up.

Prisoners found to be harboring grudges were forced to put on gloves and box each other. A guard refereed while the inmates watched.

Best often walked freely and alone throughout the prison. In many cases, however, his sleek young Doberman pinscher walked with him.

Becoming an astute politician, he convinced Governor Adams that he should report directly to him, not to a prison board of control. The Governor agreed and abolished the board.

Best shaped the prison into a burgeoning array of down-to-earth businesses—industrial shops and agriculture of all sorts. The prison industries turned out automobile license plates, road signs, shirts, socks, coats, pants, jackets, hats, rugs, and soap, just to name a few. All in all, seventy-five items were once produced—which by today's standards would never be allowed. In 1939, Best became the president of the American Association of Prison Wardens.

He was a ham and an inveterate prankster. Once when a group of livestock growers and feeders was invited to hold their meeting in the prison dining room, the warden began their meeting with a welcoming speech. While he was speaking, an anxious inmate entered the room, walked right up, and interrupted the warden. In a low distinct voice, he told the warden he was terribly upset because a certain man on the outside was "bothering around" his wife. The warden looked distressed.

"You mustn't interrupt now," the warden said. Even so, a serious dialogue continued until the inmate looked up and, shock in his voice, told the warden that the very man who was "bothering around" his wife was in this room. Then he pointed to one of the "leading cattle buyers of the west," whom he called by name. The audience gasped, but the patter between the warden and the prisoner continued until the audience discovered that it was all a prank and responded with a roar of laughter (Spring, 1945).

In later life, Best had to face trial for the mishandling of funds. Right off, he admitted he was not good with finances, that his own finances had blurred into those of the prison.

But he cooperated. He worked at explaining each situation as best he could and was acquitted.

Pasquale Marranzino, a columnist for *Rocky Mountain News,* described the businesslike side of the warden:

Perhaps Roy's greatest virtue was his willingness to take a stand—a vanishing virtue in the world of today that hides behind amendments, civil service curtains and strange beliefs that the public shouldn't know what its right hand was doing.

Newspapermen liked Roy Best because he gave them answers to their questions—even if the questions were pointed to make him look bad. When there was trouble at the pen, Roy took the blame and answered the charges. And he did it straightforward and without hesitation. . . .

There was a beautiful man-to-man relationship that Roy built up at the pen. Each knew exactly where the other stood. And each honored in the other a thing unrecognized in penitentiaries—integrity (1954).

But Best had a brutal side. He showed it on the day Joe Arridy was being interrogated in Cheyenne. The day before, five inmates, with a cache of two pistols and one hundred rounds of ammunition hidden in a wall, were foiled in their plot to kidnap the warden and use him as a hostage. When reporters asked Best what he planned to do, his answer came quickly:

"They probably will ride the old gray mare," the warden said, referring to the wooden horse in the prison yard, where unruly convicts are whipped. "She's got her tail up and rarin' to go. . . ."

Best, a heavy-set powerful man, whips mutinous prisoners himself. He said he was "too tired" from digging thru the wall to recover the firearms and cartridges to whip them today (TPC, 8-25-36).

The next day, Best did whip the would-be kidnappers with a broad leather strap. It was done with a physician present, while other inmates watched. He never hid this practice from the general public, and every man in confinement knew that if he committed an extraordinary violation of prison rules, he had a date with Roy on the "mare."

In later life, he was hauled into federal court and charged with violating the prisoners' civil rights when he flogged them. He was acquitted because he had never hidden the fact that he did it, and the state of Colorado did not have a statute that either mandated or prohibited such a practice. But there was still more to be discovered. Marranzino described a surprising tenderness as well:

I witnessed the gas-chamber execution of Bat Battalino, convicted and admitted slayer of a Denver restaurateur. Bat was a tough cookie. He threatened at every turn to strangle Best, reporters, guards, and anyone in reach.

But he met in the warden a man who laughed at his toughness. They faced each other day after day during the Bat's stay in death row. And the night Roy tripped the cyanide pellets into the crock of acid under Bat's iron chair was one of tremendous emotion.

Until the last, the Bat was snarling, insulting, vituperative. Best trumped his every play. And seconds before the execution, Bat called Roy into the death chamber and thanked him for his kindness and courtesy. They shook hands firmly, and Bat went to one of the bravest deaths anyone ever saw.

After the execution Best was shaken and pale. Tears were in his eyes and he was moody for a week. Strangely enough, he didn't believe in capital punishment (1954).

In another situation, twelve-year-old James Melton shot and killed his sixteen-year-old sister. James lived in a small house in Las Animas with his single-parent father and sister Phyllis, who tried in her fumbling way to mother her little brother.

"She was always nagging me," he said, after he had pumped five .22 caliber bullets into her body. The youngster was found guilty and given a sentence of twelve years to life, and because he was a murderer, he was sentenced to the prison in Canon City.

Upon arrival at the prison, he was fingerprinted and mugged, and then Warden Best took him by the hand and walked him out of the prison to his own home.

Hard-bitten Roy Best took over from there. He said he wouldn't allow Jimmy to spend a night inside the walls. He took him into his own home and treated him as his son. And he faced the wrath of most of Canon City when he took Jimmy to school and enrolled him.

Then when Canon City turned its back on Jimmy and wouldn't allow him to go to school with its children, Roy Best arranged for private tutors.

This was heartless Roy Best, the despotic warden who whipped naughty prisoners (Marranzino, 1954).

Jimmy "did his time" with Roy and Mabel Best as his parents, and with their Doberman pinscher as his closest friend. His tutor, Verna Wheaton, found him to be a serious, eager student. With books furnished by the local school board, she saw that he received a well-grounded education. When certain Canon City citizens warned her that he might be dangerous, her response was quick: "Bosh, I know boys" (*Life,* 1948).

❑ ❑ ❑

No matter how anyone viewed Warden Roy Best, it became clear that he cast a long shadow that covered the whole prison. On July 2, 1937, Joe Arridy was delivered to that warden, fingerprinted, "mugged," and numbered 19845. For the rest of his life, he lived under the shadow of that creative, brutal, and tender warden. And it is altogether conceivable that Joe's days in Roy Best's prison were by far the happiest days of his life.

42

SOUNDS OF JOY

When some inmates enter a death-row cell, they begin to die. They endure twenty-three-hour lock-downs; meals eaten in the cell; walking to showers with legs and wrists shackled; standing alone in a recreation yard; glaring lights all night long; guards observing and writing on charts; others watching while they pee and crap. Some guards are filled with venom, which they release only when no one is around. Other guards show care and kindness—but if they overdo it, they are transferred.

Death row can grind down a man's body and soul until what finally walks to the chamber is only a limp, listless fraction of the man he once was. In some cases, he is already mentally and emotionally dead, and the chamber is only a room used for stopping the heart and shutting off the blood.

But not Joe. He came alive on death row, and Warden Roy Best watched it happen. There was nothing in the warden's job description for doing such things, but during the eighteen months and seven days that Joe was at Canon City, Best did everything he could to help Joe blossom.

It all began when Joe was observed polishing his metal dinner plate hour after hour, until it functioned like a mirror. Then he busied himself by making faces in it and talking to himself. Warden Best brought Joe some picture books. Joe responded with laughter and began turning pages and looking at the pictures until the books fell apart. When Best brought him a pair of scissors, Joe set to work cutting out some of the faces. He hummed as he worked.

Best surprised Joe with a bright-red car, with a wind-up mechanism and battery-powered flashlight bulbs for headlights. Joe played with that car for days on end. When the batteries for the headlights wore out, Best brought fresh ones. Again and again, Joe wound it up and let it scoot across his cell floor. When it struck the bars and turned over, Joe exploded with laughter and shouted, "Car wreck, car wreck!" Since the cell lights were on all the time—making nighttime not quite different from day—that shout sometimes could be heard at two or three o'clock in the morning! One can only imagine the effect this imposed on his cell neighbors: Angelo Agnes, a wife slayer from Denver; Norman Wharton, the murderer of Detective Jack Latting of Colorado Springs; and Pete Catalana, a dope peddler and killer from Salida.

Interestingly, the Pueblo newspapers made little mention that Joe's life in Canon City had become so happy. But the other papers did. For example, after Roy and Mabel Best gave Joe a toy train during the Christmas of 1938, *Denver Post* reporter Jack Carberry described what happened:

> The minute Arridy was out of bed, he would get out his train and wind it up. Sticking his hands through the bars of his cell, he would start the train down the narrow passageway toward the end cell fifteen feet away, where Wharton is confined.
>
> "Catch it, catch it!" he would cry.
>
> Wharton would reach out and catch the train as it went by his cell door. Winding it up, he would send it back toward Arridy.
>
> Weary hour after weary hour, Wharton would keep up this game with the feeble-minded boy.
>
> "What can a fellow do? It makes the poor fellow happy," Wharton said.
>
> Sometimes Agnes or Catalana would reach out and tip the train over.
>
> Joe would shout with glee, "A wreck! A wreck! Fix the wreck," he would call.
>
> The guard—who found, probably, a thousand wrecks of Joe's train in the last week, would unlock the door leading to the corridor behind the screen [that shuts death row off from the rest of the cell block] and set the toy aright.
>
> Everybody entered the game just to keep Joe happy (Carberry, 1939b).

"Joe Arridy is the happiest man who ever lived on death row," Warden Best said to every reporter who asked about Joe. In those days, schoolyard kids pointed at other kids and shouted, "See the happy moron, he doesn't give a darn." Warden Best had none of that attitude. He spoke about Joe with respect, and he was proud that he was thriving so well in his prison.

And Joe did thrive. He was safe and secure for the first time in his life. Here, no one beat him. No one tried to manipulate him. The cell was clean, and Joe was never hungry.

Once, when Joe was granted a new sanity trial, Best took Joe off death row and may have moved him into his own home. That may have been the reason Joe knew and talked so much about Buddy Best, the eight-year-old nephew of the warden who lived with Best. The warden, of course, would have kept such a move secret, considering that Pueblo was counting the days until the second Drain murderer would be wiped off the face of the earth.

Joe's happiness was reflected in the way he received reporters. He gladly posed for them. He was less cautious and shy. His responses came in longer, more complete sentences. He voiced his preferences. For example, the following dialogue came from an interview on December 1, 1938:

> "Don't you want to be killed?"
>
> "No, I want to live. I want to live here with Warden Best."
>
> "Don't you want to go back to the home in Grand Junction?"
>
> "No, I want to get a life sentence and stay here with Warden Best," he asserted. "At the home the kids used to beat me."
>
> "Would you run away from the home if you went back there?"
>
> "If the kids were mean to me and beat me, I would. I like it here."
>
> "Would you rather be here, Joe, than to be free on the outside?"

"Yes, I want to stay here. I can't get into trouble here. But I would like to be outside to see the shows."

"What kind of shows, Joe—ones with girls in them or about cowboys?"

"Any kind, but I think I like the ones about cowboys best."

Arridy, while he talked, played with the toy train received as a Christmas present from Warden Best.

"If they don't save you, Joe, and you die Friday, what are you going to do with your train?"

"I want to take it with me."

"Won't you give it to one of the other boys?"

"I will give it to Angelo."

"That's swell," Angelo called. "I'll trade you something for it."

"Get him to trade you a gas mask for it," Wharton said. "You're going to need that, Joe."

Arridy laughed in glee, tho he obviously did not understand the "joke."

"Joe, do you remember your trial?"

Arridy thought for a long time.

"No, I don't remember."

"Don't you remember the judge and all the people in court, and what the judge said?"

"I remember what the judge said. He said he wanted to kill Joe Arridy! Is it Sunday?"

"No, Joe, Friday, if they don't do something."

"But they will do something," Joe said hopefully.

Beyond his trial—the sentence of death by the court—Arridy could not remember.

"Do you remember after the little girls were killed, you ran away on a train, and they arrested you up in Cheyenne, Wyo?"

"No, I don't remember that. But I remember the judge wanted to kill me."

"You know what it means to go to the gas house, don't you, Joe?"

"Yes, they kill you there. But I don't want to be killed. I want a life sentence and stay here all the time."

"You like it here, Joe?"

"I never get in trouble here, and Angelo is nice to me. Maybe if I don't take my train with me, I'll give it to Angelo" (TDP, 1-1-39).

Joe did not fully understand death or execution, or a life sentence, or a judge wanting to kill him. He was getting that from his fellow inmates, who tried repeatedly to explain what they had been reading about him in the papers. They tried to help Joe understand that officials in Fremont County—the county that included the prison—were suddenly fighting for him. Those officials claimed that Joe was now their citizen, and they had the right to determine whether or not he was insane. Pueblo County vehemently disagreed, claiming it had jurisdiction over Joe, and it was their officials who should decide whether Joe should have another lunacy hearing.

The judge in the Canon City courtroom might, just *might* rule him insane and sentence him to a full and happy life in prison. But Joe's friends obviously got through to him that there was, indeed, a judge who—if he had his way—would kill him. And that judge was in Pueblo.

But all that talk really did not sink in. For example, one year earlier, on Friday, November 19, 1937, Joe did almost die. It was to be his last day. The many steps in the death ritual had begun: A pig had already been killed in the gas chamber to make sure that everything was working properly for the evening execution; plans were being made for the last visits and the last meal and the last march. Then Joe received a stay. His response was recorded in an evening paper:

> A toy automobile provided more joy and amusement Friday for Joe Arridy than notification that a last-minute order of the Colorado Supreme Court had saved him from the state's lethal gas chamber, at least temporarily.
>
> Arridy, an illiterate and a former inmate of the State Home for Mental Defectives, displayed no emotion whatever when he was notified Friday by Roy Best, warden of the state penitentiary in Canon City, and Rev. Albert Schaller, the Catholic prison chaplain, that he had been given a new lease on life.
>
> It was evident that Arridy did not fully realize just what the Supreme Court action was all about. He thanked Warden Best and Father Schaller, and then continued playing with the red toy automobile that has provided his only amusement during his long confinement (Osborne, 1937).

That was vintage Joe. He just kept on playing with the car. He had found his place. He wasn't concerned. Warden Best would take care of everything.

43

IRELAND

Warden Best was working quietly to save his toy-loving friend's life. By law, wardens aren't supposed to do such things. Their job is merely to carry out the punishment orders of the courts—no more and no less. So he may have been forced to pressure the Grand Junction home superintendent to make some moves for him, even though Superintendent Jefferson made statements to the press that might not have squared with the warden's. Jefferson still believed that Joe was a walking piece of diseased germ plasma, and he may not have given Joe the same respect the warden did. To Best, Joe was simply Joe.

But in Jefferson's educated way, he moaned to the press, "They won't give me a sterilization law or anything else, but these defectives are my children. I have to do what I can for them. No one else will" (Osborne, 1937). One way or the other, the superintendent chose—or was booted into finding—a lawyer: Ireland.

Gail L. Ireland, in his own way, was as refreshingly unorthodox as Warden Roy Best. Both Ireland and Best were leading lights in Colorado's current political scene. Later, Best would run for governor and lose, but Ireland would run for Attorney General and win by a mere 204 votes.

Up to this point, Ireland was an irrigation lawyer, but he was a winning one. Two of his cases went to the United States Supreme Court. In one, he successfully ended a 42-year dispute between Colorado and Kansas over the proper use of water in the Arkansas River. In the second, he won in Colorado's bitter dispute with Nebraska and Wyoming over the North Platte River (Hansen, 1952). He also was touted "as a sort of Johnny Appleseed, scattering the gospel of citizenship responsibility. He believes this type of citizenship is vitally needed as a cover crop against further erosion of America's topsoil of freedom" (Hansen, 1952). Consequently, he took many pro-bono pursuits as a good citizen. He called them "labors of love."

Ireland managed to gain nine stays of execution for Joe. All were based on the same old legal question—whether or not Joe was insane. It was the only legal plank available in those days. With each stay, Ireland seemed to come closer to saving Joe's life. Each time, he tried a new and different attack. As Joe's final date with death approached, Ireland worked harder. His commitment was evident in his letter to Dr. Jefferson on November 17, 1938:

My Dear Doc:
　　Well, Joe is safe again. I wasn't sure that I could work this last-minute procedure, but it

worked, and now we have to get busy and use every possible thing we can think of to get a commutation to a life sentence. . . . At least we have a breathing spell again, and so has Arridy.

Some time ago, I wrote you, but never got an answer from you. . . . In case you do not know what has happened, I will give you a brief outline.

I made arrangements to have a resident of repute of Fremont County swear to a lunacy petition at Canon City. Fortunately, I was able to get Abbott Schwinn, the head of the Holy Cross Abbey at Canon City. He is, as I understand it, next to Bishop Vehr in rank among Catholic clergy in Colorado. Therefore, his name means a great deal. Then I went down yesterday and argued the matter before Judge Eldred, [Fremont] County Judge. The Attorney General's Office sent the Deputy Attorney General down to resist my move, but the Judge finally held with me and said that he had jurisdiction. I spent a lot of time with Roy Best and his sympathy is all with us. . . .

The Attorney General will file a petition tomorrow asking that the Supreme Court issue a Writ of Prohibition forbidding the County Court of Fremont to proceed further until the question of jurisdiction is settled. . . .

If the Supreme Court holds that I have started the lunacy proceeding in the wrong forum, then I will have to file in Pueblo County in the District Court, which I don't want to do if I can help it. However, if I do, then I will petition for a change of venue if the District Attorney asks for a jury. In any event we are not yet licked.

You will remember that when you first asked me to take on this job, I told you I would stay with you until the last dog was hung. I still mean it, and with your help, we will show these people who are actuated by passion and prejudice that they cannot always get away with it. If Arridy had actually participated in the crime of murder, I would not feel as I do, but since the evidence in the case, as well as all the confessions of Aguilar, clear him of any such connection, I feel that you and I are doing the State of Colorado a real service if we can keep it from committing a murder itself. Believe me when I say that if he is gassed, it will take a long time for the State of Colorado to live down the disgrace. . . .

Please let me hear from you at your earliest convenience. . . .

Sincerely yours,

Gail L. Ireland (CSA, 1938)

It was this Fremont-County-versus-Pueblo-County battle that Joe's fellow inmates were trying to explain to him. This latest move came as a surprise. After the well-known Leonard Schwinn, the abbot of Holy Cross abbey at Canon City, filed for a sanity hearing, Fremont County Judge Kent L. Eldred held a jurisdictional hearing on November 16. Roy Best attended that hearing "and made no secret of his hope that Arridy's life will be spared" (TDP, 11-16-38). Eldred ruled that his court in Canon City had jurisdiction over Joe. The judge appointed two psychiatrists to evaluate Joe, and he set a date for the sanity hearing. The doctors said that they would move quickly on the order.

As soon as Judge Eldred ruled that he had jurisdiction, Colorado's assistant attorney general, Reid Williams, rushed back to the state Supreme Court in Denver and filed a writ of prohibition, asking the court to stop Eldred from carrying out his plan.

Ireland rushed back to Denver, too, and was present in the Supreme Court when Williams filed his writ. He, in the presence of Williams, filed an application to the Supreme

Court, asking it to postpone the death dates for Arridy until all the legal questions were solved.

Later, Ireland told the press, "We were afraid to go into Pueblo County, because there already were two 'hometown' verdicts against us there. There's no use trying to get justice in that atmosphere" (TDP, 11-16-38).

The Supreme Court granted a stay until January 2, 1939. In the meantime, it would study all issues related to Joe. It took its time. Then just before the end of 1938, the court ruled that only Pueblo County had jurisdiction over Joe Arridy.

Ireland announced that he would file for a sanity hearing in Pueblo County Court. But before he filed, Pueblo County Judge Harry Leddy made an unprecedented move. On Saturday, December 31—the morning of New Year's Eve—he traveled to Canon City and demanded to see Joe for himself. Since he had presided over both of Joe's trials in Pueblo, he wanted to see if there had been any changes in him. He talked to Joe for fifteen minutes and left.

That afternoon, Ireland filed for a sanity hearing in the Pueblo County Court.

On Monday, January 2, 1939, Judge Leddy denied Ireland's petition. He based his rejection on his own visit with Joe: "I find no change in his condition, and therefore he is sane now," the judge said (TDP, 1-3-39).

Joe was scheduled to die on Friday evening, January 6.

44

HOLY WEEK

Judge Harry Leddy's sudden moves set off a series of wildly aimed roman-candle shots by those wanting Joe to live. *The Denver Post* published an attractive front-page picture of Warden Roy Best with his hat pushed back, leaning close to Joe, looking him right in the eye. Joe is hunched down with his elbows on his knees, smiling warmly into Best's face. The photo's caption:

Only a few days of life were left for Joe Arridy Tuesday, after Judge Harry Leddy of Pueblo refused his plea for a new hearing on his sanity and decreed that his death sentence, for the sex murder of Dorothy Drain, 15, of Pueblo should be carried out on schedule. Below, Warden Roy Best (right) is seen in the cell which Arridy has occupied in death row at the penitentiary at Canon City for nearly two years, telling the prisoner of his probable fate next Friday night when he is due to walk the last long mile to the lethal gas chamber. While Arridy told Best he understood "the judge wants to kill me," he showed no emotion and, a moment later, laughed and joked with the warden—AP Photo (TDP, 13-39).

Attorney Ireland bounced back by telling the reporters that Judge Leddy had "evaded the issue":

I have not read the order in full. The court clerk read it to me over the telephone. If it is as I believed it to be, I will go into the supreme court Wednesday and ask that body to intervene. . . .
   Judge Leddy's order, as I understand it, does not say he is free from doubt. It simply throws the whole matter back on the Pueblo jury—a home town jury—which originally declared this imbecile to be sane (TDP, 1-3-39).

WEDNESDAY

Ireland moved quickly in two directions. He appealed to Governor Teller Ammons to commute Joe's sentence to life in prison. And he petitioned the Supreme Court for a stay of execution and asked it to order another sanity hearing in Pueblo.
   Father Albert Schaller, the prison chaplain, stated that he would employ "ministrations to a child about to die."

Because he assertedly does not realize his impending doom, and may not do so even on the night of his execution, it is indicated that Father Schaller will probably administer the last rites of the Roman Catholic Church to Arridy in the manner in which they usually are given to a child below the age of reasoning.

Father Albert has made repeated attempts to impress the approach of death on Arridy's mind in recent days, but has failed on each occasion. . . .

Arridy's continued response to statements he is going to die is a laugh, and sometimes the words, "No, no, not me." Warden Roy Best of the prison has reported: "He cannot comprehend that the state wants to take his life" (TPC, 1-5).

When Warden Best asked Joe if there was anything he wanted, his response was quick: "Cigars and candy."

Warden Best told the press that no outsiders would be allowed to attend Joe's execution. It would be the smallest number ever to see an official execution in Colorado, Best said (TDR, 1-7). The only observers would be the official witnesses and authorized newspaper people. He announced that no pig would be killed to test the chamber. He told reporters that he was leaving Canon City until the night of the execution. But he didn't leave. He stayed in the prison area. Quite often, he was with Joe.

A Canon City reporter described the usual tense rush of workmen making preparation for Friday evening's event. He contrasted that frenzy with Joe, who "sat in his cell making faces in his polished tin dinner plate—unmindful of the fate that is to befall him in two days" (TDR, 1-4).

THURSDAY

The warden asked Joe what he wanted to eat for his last meal. His answer: "Ice cream."

Attorney Ireland and four others were granted an eleventh-hour meeting with Governor Teller Ammons. The presenters: Abbott Leonard Schwinn of Holy Cross Abbey in Canon City; Dr. H. A. LaMoure, superintendent of the State Home for Mental Defectives at Ridge; Denver psychiatrist Leo V. Tepley, who offered to evaluate Joe free of charge. Dr. Ben Jefferson of the Grand Junction home was also there, and for one last time, gave his now-famous "Joe-is-one-of-my-children-and-he-belongs-in-my-institution" speech.

While Ireland was making his plea, the governor interrupted. "Gail, you cannot say, can you, that Arridy has not had the fullest protection of his rights that the law allows."

Ireland admitted that the case had been considered by the Pueblo District Court and the Colorado Supreme Court, but contended that the Pueblo juries were forced to act "in a community aroused to a high pitch of passion and prejudice." He then added that "the state law forbidding execution of an idiot [a label that didn't quite fit Joe] was more plain than the statute prohibiting the death penalty of an insane person."

The five men—grasping at every straw—insisted that Arridy "merely stood by" while Frank Aguilar murdered the girl. Tepley reinforced the statement by saying, "Imbeciles of Arridy's class were purely mechanical in action." After the meeting, the governor remarked to reporters, "There was no one here to argue for the girl" (RMN, 1-6).

Warden Best brought Joe a package of cigars and a box of candy made by Mabel Best. When Joe received them, he gave a cheer and began to munch on the candy. Then he lit a cigar, got sick, and had to lie down for an hour. He gave the rest of his candy away.

It was reported that Governor Ammons was still deliberating late in the evening.

FRIDAY

Mabel Best had made a three-gallon freezer of ice cream, and the warden ordered that Joe should have ice cream with all three meals. Joe started with a breakfast that consisted only of ice cream.

Governor Ammons announced that he was still pondering the Arridy situation.

The battery for the headlight on Joe's train had burned out. The warden went down town, purchased a battery, and put it in Joe's locomotive.

Warden Best had planned a surprise for Joe by arranging for his mother, Mary Arridy, to come for a visit. Joe's father had died eleven months earlier. Mrs. Arridy and three others arrived in the late morning. As soon as she exited the car, she began to moan. Reporter Jack Carberry described the actual meeting:

> His dull, bewildered silence turned a meeting with his mother, Mrs. Mary Arridy, into a strange, frightening interlude, much more awesome to observers than if he had broken down and wept.
>
> It was only the second time Mrs. Arridy had visited Joe since he was taken to the penitentiary. With her were her daughter, Amelia Arridy, 14; Joe's aunt, Mrs. Helen Marguerite; and a cousin, Christine Marguerite [also 14].
>
> They had been brought to the penitentiary by Sheriff Lewis Worker of Pueblo County and were ushered into the anteroom in the penitentiary offices by Warden Best and Father Schaller. The moment Mrs. Arridy saw her son she burst into tears.
>
> "My Joe!" she exclaimed. "My Joe!"
>
> She threw her arms about him and would have fallen to her knees in front of him, had he not awkwardly supported her.
>
> "Hello," he muttered, turning his face toward a wall. His eyes were not even damp.
>
> For more than fifteen minutes the group sat in the room, and during all the time, there was not a sound except the sobbing of Mrs. Arridy. Joe made no effort to speak, and his relatives just looked at him.
>
> His expression changed only when a group of trusties walked in with a meal Best had ordered for Joe and his visitors. There was a slight smile when he saw the three-gallon ice-cream freezer.
>
> Best and Father Schaller tried several times to lighten the tension in the room, to ease the fear and dismay in the eyes of Joe's mother, aunt, and cousin, but it was no use. All but Mrs. Arridy remained painfully apathetic (Carberry, 1939*a*).

When the warden said it was time to end the visit, Mrs. Arridy again began to cry. As she left the room, she started to scream. That shrieking could be heard throughout the prison, and it didn't stop until she was placed in Sheriff Worker's car.

Joe immediately went back to his cell. He filled the rest of his day busily playing with his toy train. He stopped only to visit when the chaplain came in to help him practice the "Our Father" and rosary, or when the warden dropped in. Then it was back to his train.

Warden Best waited in his office from 4:00 until 5:00 P.M. for a call from the governor.

Shortly after 5:00 P.M., the warden received a call from the Colorado Supreme Court. They had just come together in a special session to consider a petition from attorney Ireland—to decide one more time whether Joe was sane or insane, whether he knew right from wrong, whether he lived or died.

At 6:00 P.M., Best received a call from Governor Ammons, who ordered that the execution be held up until the Supreme Court made a decision.

At 6:15, the Supreme Court called. The court had voted 4-3 that Ireland's petition be denied. Joe Arridy lost by one vote.

Governor Ammons called ten minutes later. He told Best that he would not grant clemency. He ordered the warden to carry out the execution.

45

GOOD-BYE, JOE

Joe's last meal was taken with Father Schaller. It was a bowl of ice cream. Then Father Schaller gave Joe last rites:

Father Schaller prepared Joe for death in the manner of his church dealing with a child about to die. He recited prayers and asked Joe to pray after him.

"We'll say the Our Father," Father Schaller said. "Now, Joe, you follow me—say what I say."

"Our Father," said Father Schaller.

"Our Father," said Joe.

"Who art," intoned the priest.

"Who art," repeated Joe.

You see, Joe Arridy couldn't remember the full line, "Our Father, who art in Heaven." He had to repeat it two words at a time. That was Joe Arridy's mentality.

The priest said his church's "Hail Mary" the same way.

Then he talked to Joe as a father might talk to his little son (Carberry, 1939c).

When the priest finished, Joe returned to his train.

Soon, the warden and the chaplain came for Joe for the last time.

Best read the death warrant in Joe's cell.

Joe sat on his bunk. He did not know what the words were. He did know, however, what they meant.

"Do you understand, Joe?" Best asked.

"They are killing me," Joe said, never changing his expression.

"We are ready," Father Schaller said (Carberry, 1939c).

Joe wanted to take his train with him, but he had been talked out of it. He gave it to Angelo Agnes. He gave his shiny plate to the warden. He asked the warden to give the red car to his nephew, Buddy Best. Although everyone—especially the warden, the chaplain, and his cell neighbors—had tried to explain dying, Joe at least understood that he couldn't take any of his treasures with him.

The warden suggested that he say good-bye to his friends. He stopped in front of each cell and gave each man some of the remaining cigars. He shook their hands, and smiled.

Agnes and Catalana could not bring themselves to speak. But Wharton did: "Keep your chin up, Joe. I'll be meeting you."

With the chaplain on his right and the warden on his left, Joe walked outside where fifty "authorized" witnesses were waiting. Riley Drain was not among them. They assembled behind the three for the long hike up the gravel road to the top of Woodpecker Hill. Every prison window that fronted onto the gravel road contained a man watching as the procession moved along. Over the crunching of gravel, the witnesses struggled to hear the conversation between Joe and his two escorts.

The warden asked Joe whether he still planned to raise chickens in heaven. Joe had got that idea from listening to the other inmates talk about their future and had decided that chickens would be fine.

But now he said, "No, I want to play the harp like Father Schaller told me I could." After Father Schaller had administered the last rites, he had tried to tell Joe what heaven would be like and had included a story about playing harps. After that, chickens were out and harps were in.

When they approached the small bungalow-like building with the bay windows, Joe entered the backdoor while the witnesses assembled in front of the windows. According to the January 7 *Chieftain:*

> The doomed youth was grinning as he entered the gas chamber and prison officials began preparing him for execution in a small room off the steel execution chamber.
>
> While Arridy's prison-style blue shirt and pants were removed, Father Schaller and Arridy repeated the Lord's Prayer once more—still with just two words at a time.
>
> Arridy stepped into the gas chamber still grinning, and immediately sat down in the second of the three chairs in the small room. He was clad only in a pair of white shorts and socks.
>
> The grin left his face when the black bandage was placed over his eyes. He seemed puzzled, but the grin returned when Warden Best took his hand and reassured him.
>
> The guards then proceeded to quickly strap him into the chair. His arms and legs were drawn tight to the steel chair, and a wide belt was strapped across his chest and caught behind the chair. Then all the officials left the execution chamber except Father Schaller, who with tears in his eyes, took Arridy's hand and bid him good-bye.
>
> Then the priest left the chamber and the steel door was closed.

REFERENCES

Arridy v Colorado (1938). *Joe Arridy v The People of the State of Colorado.* Colorado Supreme Court, Case No. 14260. Denver, Colorado.

Brigham, Carl C. (1923). *A Study of American Intelligence.* Princeton: Princeton University Press.

Carberry, Jack (1939a). "Arridy Gives Up His Toys as Death Nears." *The Denver Post,* January 6.

Carberry, Jack (1939b). "Arridy Dies in Gas Chamber." *The Denver Post,* January 7.

Carberry, Jack (1939c). "Ax Slayer Becomes Unconscious After First Few Breaths." *The Denver Post,* January 8.

Carrel, Alexis (1935). *Man: The Unknown.* New York: Harper & Brothers.

Chase, Allan (1990). *The Legacy of Malthus: The Social Costs of the New Scientific Racism.* Urbana: University of Illinois Press.

Cheyenne Eagle (1961). "Carroll Services Saturday." *Cheyenne Eagle,* May 19.

Clarity, James F. (1995). "When the 'Hungry Fiend' Was Loose in Ireland." *The New York Times,* February 20.

Clark, Norman H. (1976). *Deliver Us from Evil: An Interpretation of American Prohibition.* New York: Norton.

Cless, Ralph (1939). "Joe Arridy Pays His Debt to Society—Lethal Gas Erases Grin." *The Pueblo Chieftain,* January 7.

Colorado State Home and Training School for Mental Defectives—Sixth Biennial Report (1931). Grand Junction, Colorado: For the Years 1929–1930 and six months of 1931.

Colorado v Arrdy (1937). *The People of the State of Colorado v Joe Arrdy.* Pueblo District Court, Case No. 24733. Pueblo, Colorado.

Cooke, Alistair (1975). *Alistair Cooke's America.* New York: Alfred A. Knopf.

CPP. Capital Punishment Project. Drawer 277, Headland, Alabama 36345.

Crissey, Marie Skodak. (1983). "The Searchlight of Science." *Education and Training of the Mentally Retarded.*

CSA. Colorado State Archives, 1313 Sherman Street, Denver, Colorado.

Daniel, Clifton (1987). *Chronicle of the 20th Century.* Mt. Kisko, New York: Chronicle Publications.

Davenport, Charles B. (1911). *Heredity in Relation to Eugenics.* New York: Henry Holt & Company.

Dodds, Joanne (1995). Personal correspondence, May 8, 1995.

Everington, Caroline T, and Luckasson, Ruth (1992). *Competence Assessment for Standing Trial for Defendants with Mental Retardation (CAST/MR).* Worthington, Ohio: International Diagnostic Systems (I.D.S.).

Gideon v. Wainwright (1963). United States Supreme Court (372 U.S. 335).

Goddard, Henry Herbert (1912). *The Kallikak Family.* New York: The MacMillan Company.

Goddard, Henry Herbert (1913). "The Binet Tests in Relation to Immigration." *Journal of Psycho-asthenics* 18:105-107.

Goffman, Erving (1961). *Asylums—Essays on the Social Situation of Mental Patients and Other Inmates.* New York: Doubleday Anchor Books.

Gould, Stephen Jay (1981). *The Mismeasure of Man.* New York: W. W. Norton.

Grady, J. Arthur (1936). "The Maniac Murder of Dorothy Drain." *Official Detective,* Vol. 11, No. 12. November 1.

Grant, Madison (1916). *The Passing of the Great Race.* New York: Charles Scribner's Sons.

Grand, Madison (1921). "Restriction of Immigration: Racial Aspects." *Journal of National Institute of Science,* 6:1-11.

Guest, Clifford (1936a). "Sheriff's Keen Wit Revealed." *The Pueblo Chieftain,* August 29.

Guest, Clifford (1936b). "Pueblo Officers Were on Right Track." *The Pueblo Chieftain,* September 3.

Hansen, Mark (1952). "Gail Ireland Champions Underdog, Americanism." *The Denver Post,* March 3.

Hitler, Adolf (1962). *Mein Kampf,* trans. R. Manheim. New York: Houghton.

Kamin, Leon J. (1976). "Heredity, Politics, and Psychology II." Block, N.J., and Dworkin, Gerald (eds.) *The IQ Controversy.* New York: Random House (Pantheon).

LHC. Local History Center of the Public Library, 516 Macon, Canon City, Colorado.

LIFE (1948). "Warden Adopts Young Murderer." *Life Magazine,* April 12.

Marranzino, Pasquale (1954). "No Sponge in Roy's Corner." *The Denver Post,* May 28.

McElvaine, Robert S. (1985). *The Great Depression: America, 1921–1941.* New York: Times Books.

Miranda v. Arizona (1966). United States Supreme Court (384 U.S. 436).

Mosely, Leonard (1976). *Lindbergh: A Biography.* New York: Doubleday & Company, Inc.

MWC. Museum of Western Colorado, Regional History Division, 248 S. 4th Street, Grand Junction, Colorado.

O'Brien, Charles T. (1937). "Court Order Stays Arridy's Execution." *The Denver Post,* November 19.

Osborne, Harold (1936). "Aguilar Signs Confession." *The Pueblo Chieftain,* September 3.

Osborne, Harold (1937). "Frank Aguilar Executed for Brutal Crime." *The Pueblo Chieftain,* August 14.

PLDA. Pueblo Library, District Archives, 100 E. Abriendo Avenue, Pueblo, Colorado.

Perske, Robert (1991). *Unequal Justice? What Can Happen When Persons with Retardation or Other Developmental Disabilities Encounter the Criminal Justice System.* Nashville: Abingdon Press.

Perske, Robert (1994a). "Johnny Doesn't Belong in Jail." *The Kansas City Star,* Vol. 114, No. 156, February 20.

Perske, Robert (1994b). "Thoughts on the Police Interrogation of Individuals with Mental Retardation." *Mental Retardation,* October.

Ripley, William Z. (1899). *The Races of Europe.* [Quoted in Torrey, 1992, p. 42]

RMN. *Rocky Mountain News,* Denver, Colorado.

Rust-Tierney, Diann and Wicks, Karima (1993). *Double Justice—A Documentary Film About Race and the Death Penalty.* Washington: American Civil Liberties Union—Capital Punishment Project.

Smith, J. David. (1985). *Minds Made Feeble: The Myth and Legacy of the Kallikaks.* Austin: Pro-Ed, Inc.

Spring, A. W. (1945). "Best Makes Good." *True Detective,* March 25.

TDP. *The Denver Post.* Denver, Colorado

TDR. *The Canon City Daily Record.* Canon City, Colorado.

TDS. *The Daily Sentinel.* Grand Junction, Colorado.

TPC. *The Pueblo Chieftain.* Pueblo, Colorado.

Terman, Lewis M. (1916). "The Stanford Revision of the Benet-Simon Tests," *The Measurement of Intelligence*. New York: Houghton Mifflin Co.

Torrey, E. Fuller (1992). *Freudian Fraud: The Malignant Effect of Freud's Theory on American Thought and Culture*. New York: HarperCollins.

Trent, James W., Jr. (1994). *Inventing the Feeble Mind: A History of Mental Retardation in the United States*. Berkeley: University of California Press.

Voorhees, Richard (1992). Correspondence, including the poem, "The Clinic." March 28.

Walker, Francis A. (1896). "Restriction of Immigration," *Atlantic Monthly*, June, 822-29.

WHD. Western History Department, Denver Public Library, 1357 Broadway, Denver, Colorado.

WGBH/TV (1989). "The Great Air Race of 1924." *The American Experience Series*. Boston: WGBH Educational Foundation. Air Date on the Public Broadcasting System: October 3, 1989.

Woods, Frederick A. (1906). *Mental and Moral Heredity in Royalty*. [Quoted in Torrey, 1992, p. 42.]

Woods, William H. (1951). *Report on the Winfield Training School*. Winfield, Kansas: A Report by the Acting Superintendent.

White, Bob (1936a). "Youth Confesses Pueblo Sex Slaying." *Wyoming State Leader*, August 27.

White, Bob (1936b). "Bloody Shirt Found Here—New Clue in Arrdy Case." *Wyoming State Leader*. August 31.

WSA. Wyoming State Archives, Main Library, Cheyenne, Wyoming.

WST. *Wyoming State Tribune*, Cheyenne, Wyoming.

Yerkes, Robert M. (1921). Psychological Examining in the United States Army. *Memoirs of the National Academy for Sciences*, vol. 15, 890 pp.

Young, Marguerite (1944). "The Clinic." In *Moderate Fable*. New York: Reynal & Hitchcock.

INDEX